TIGER

Adult Coloring Book

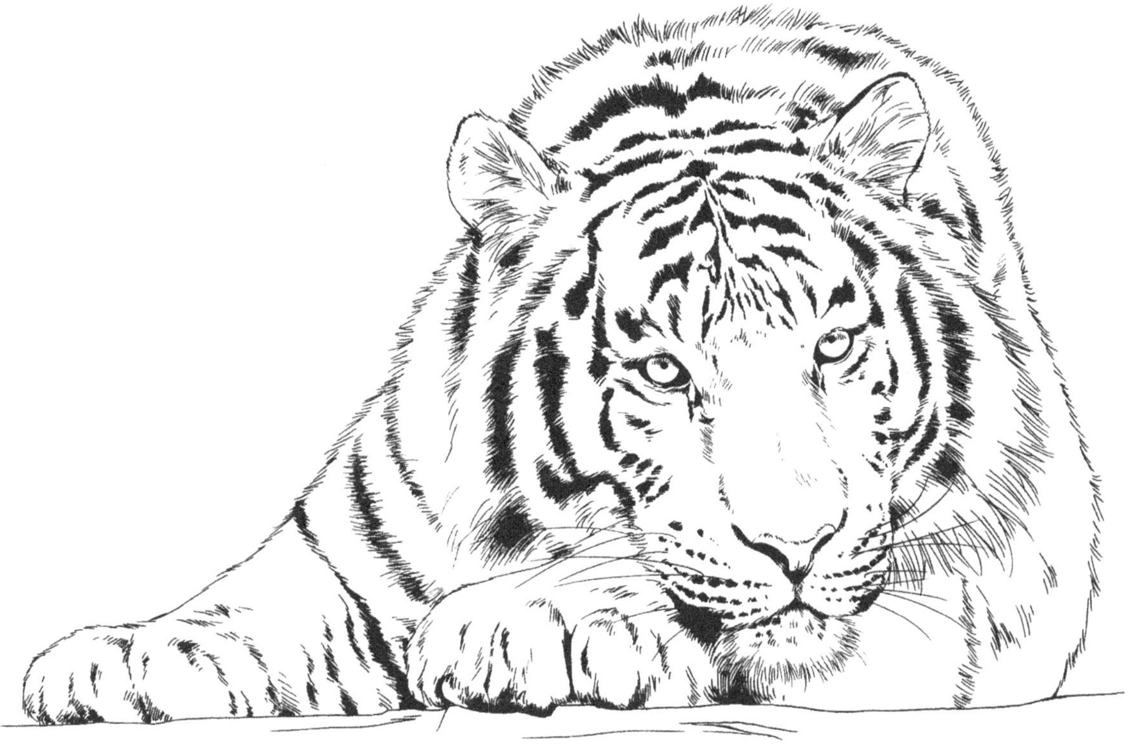

DYLANNA
Press

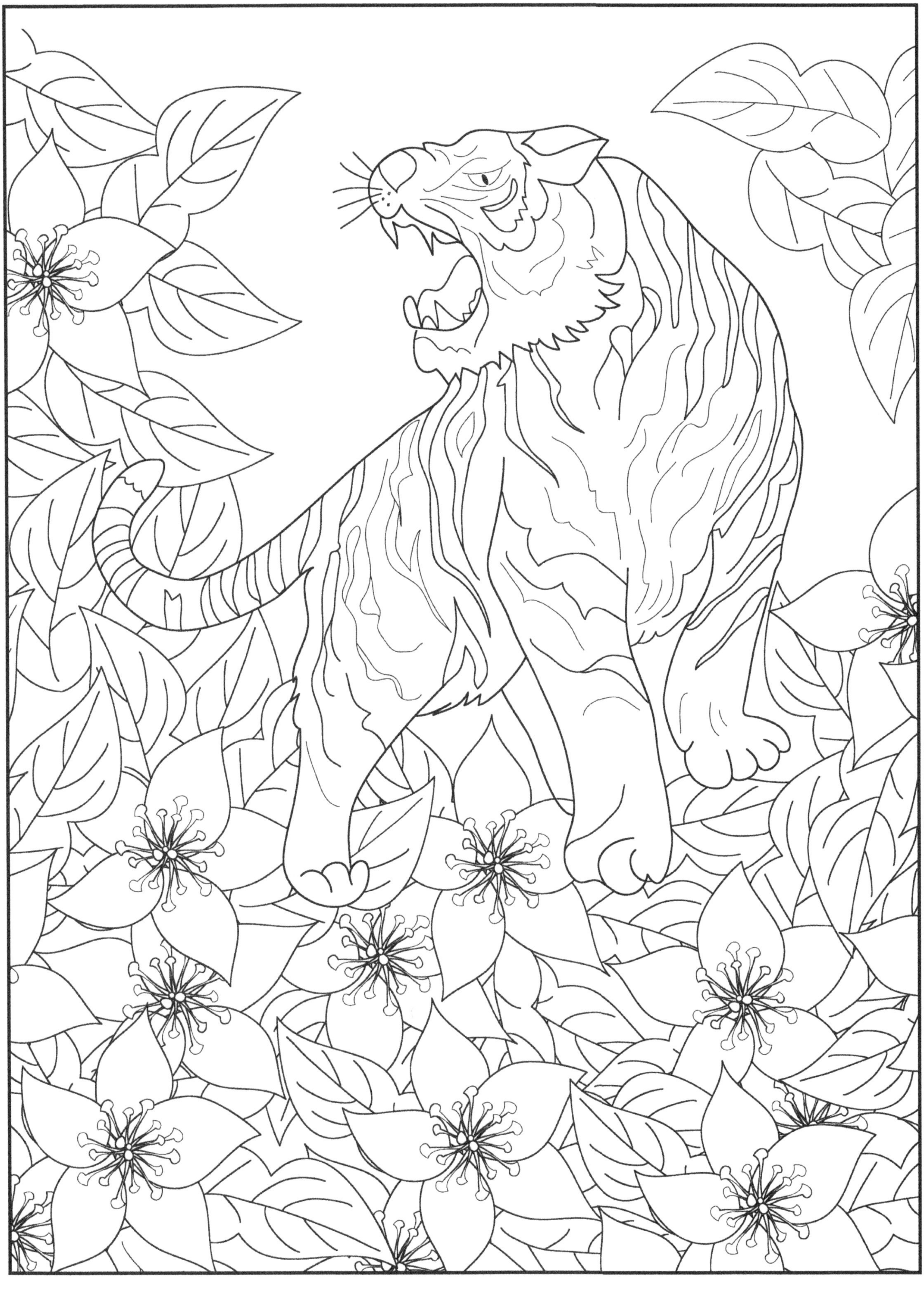

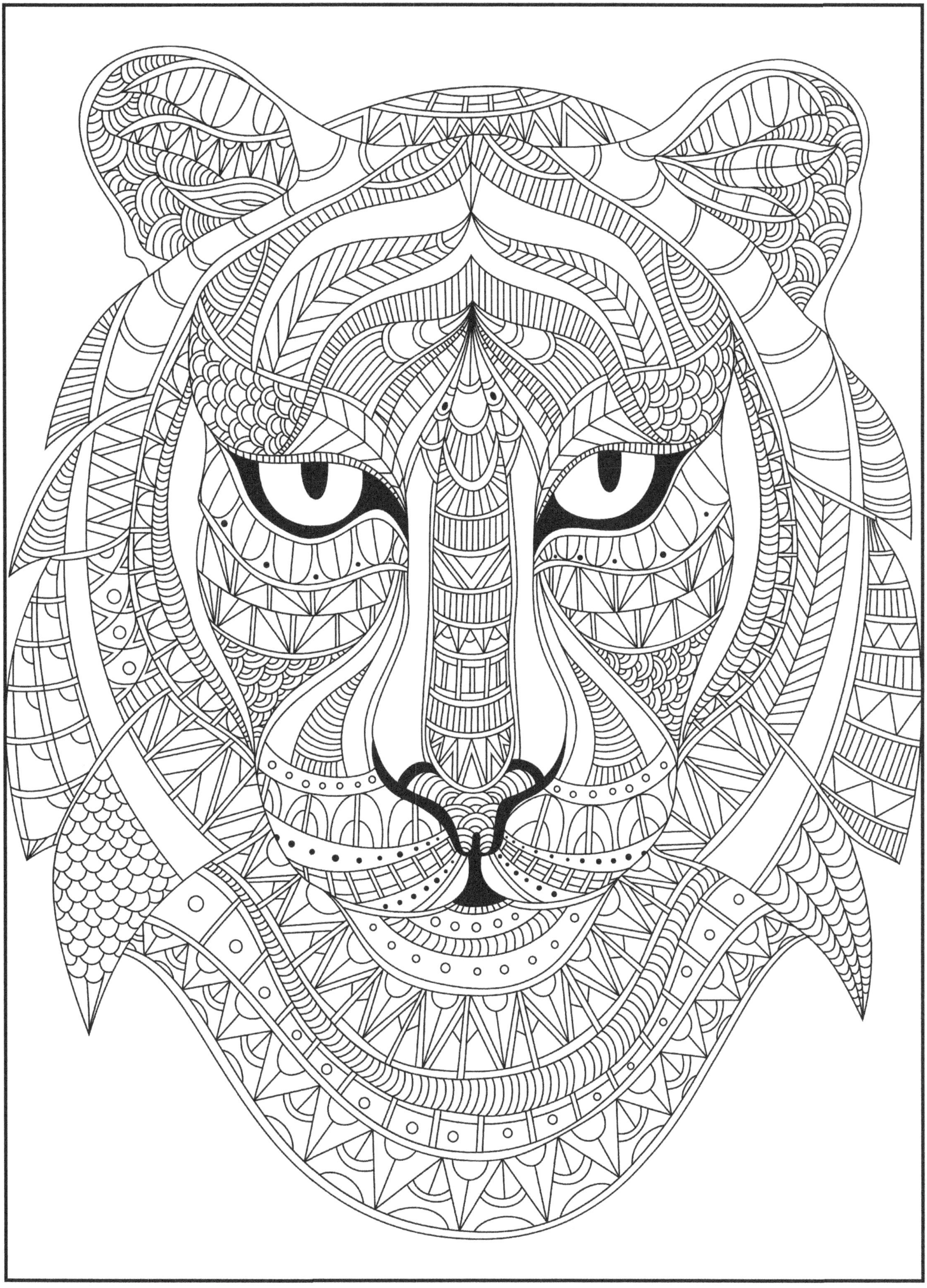

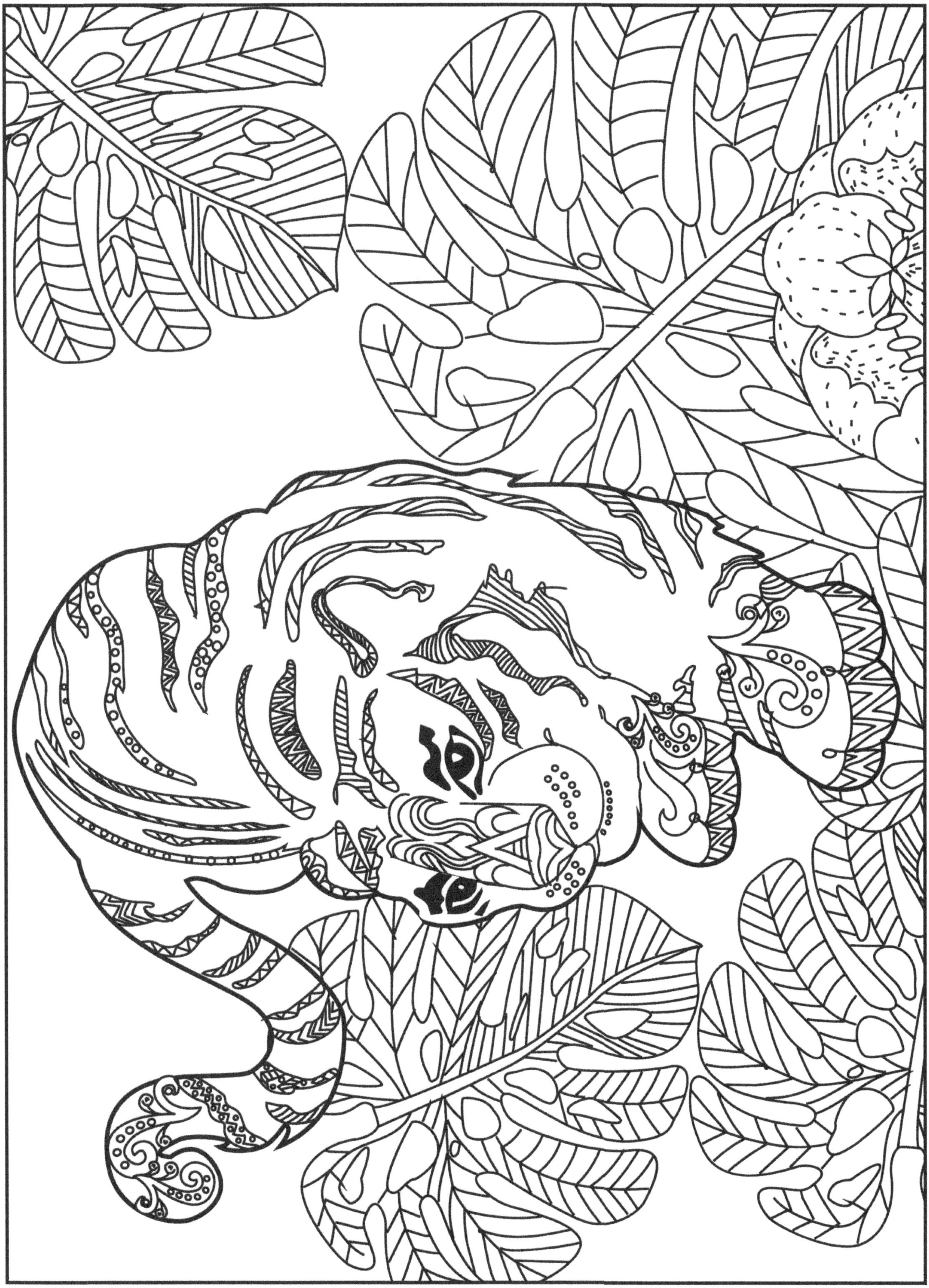

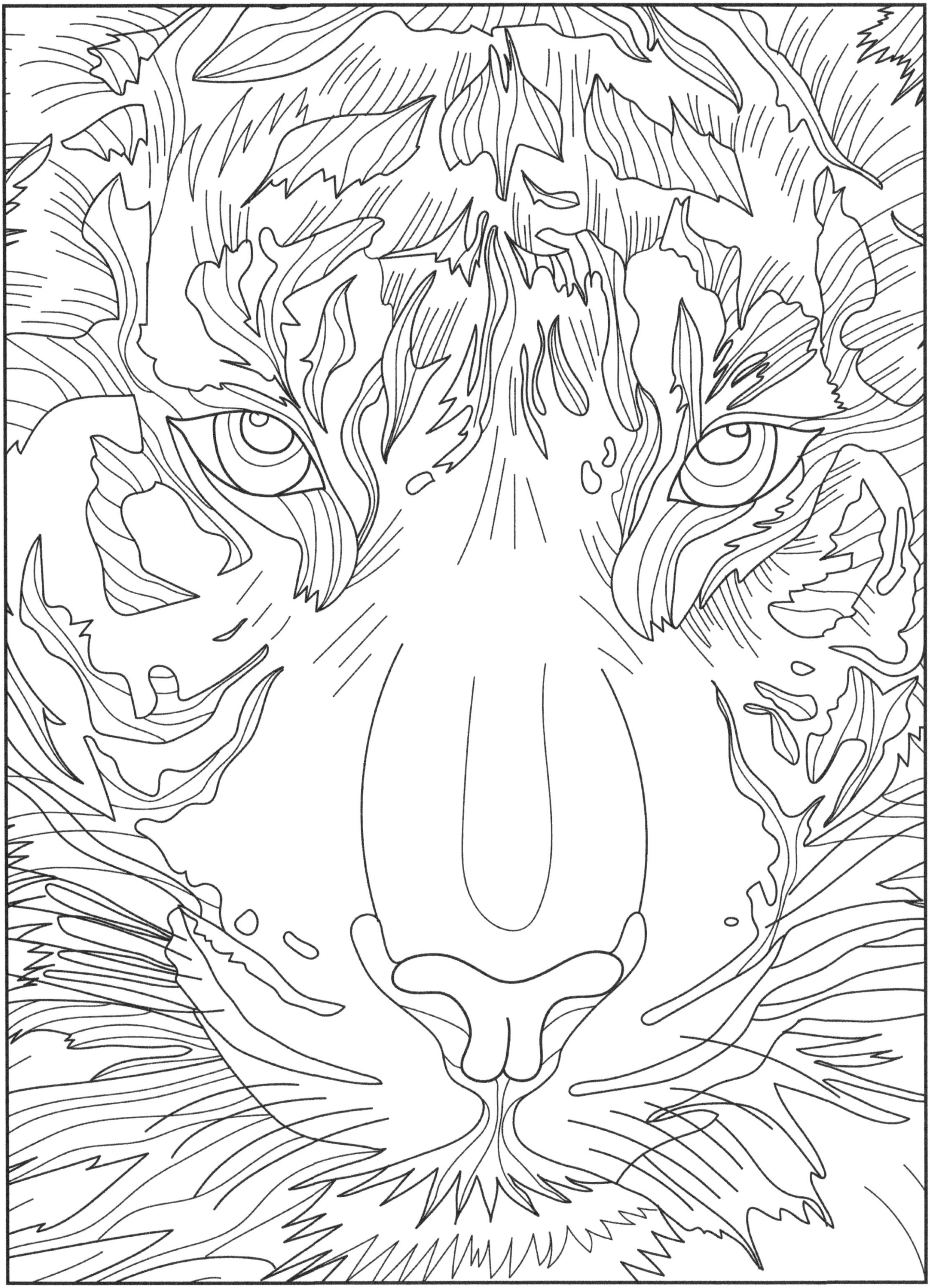

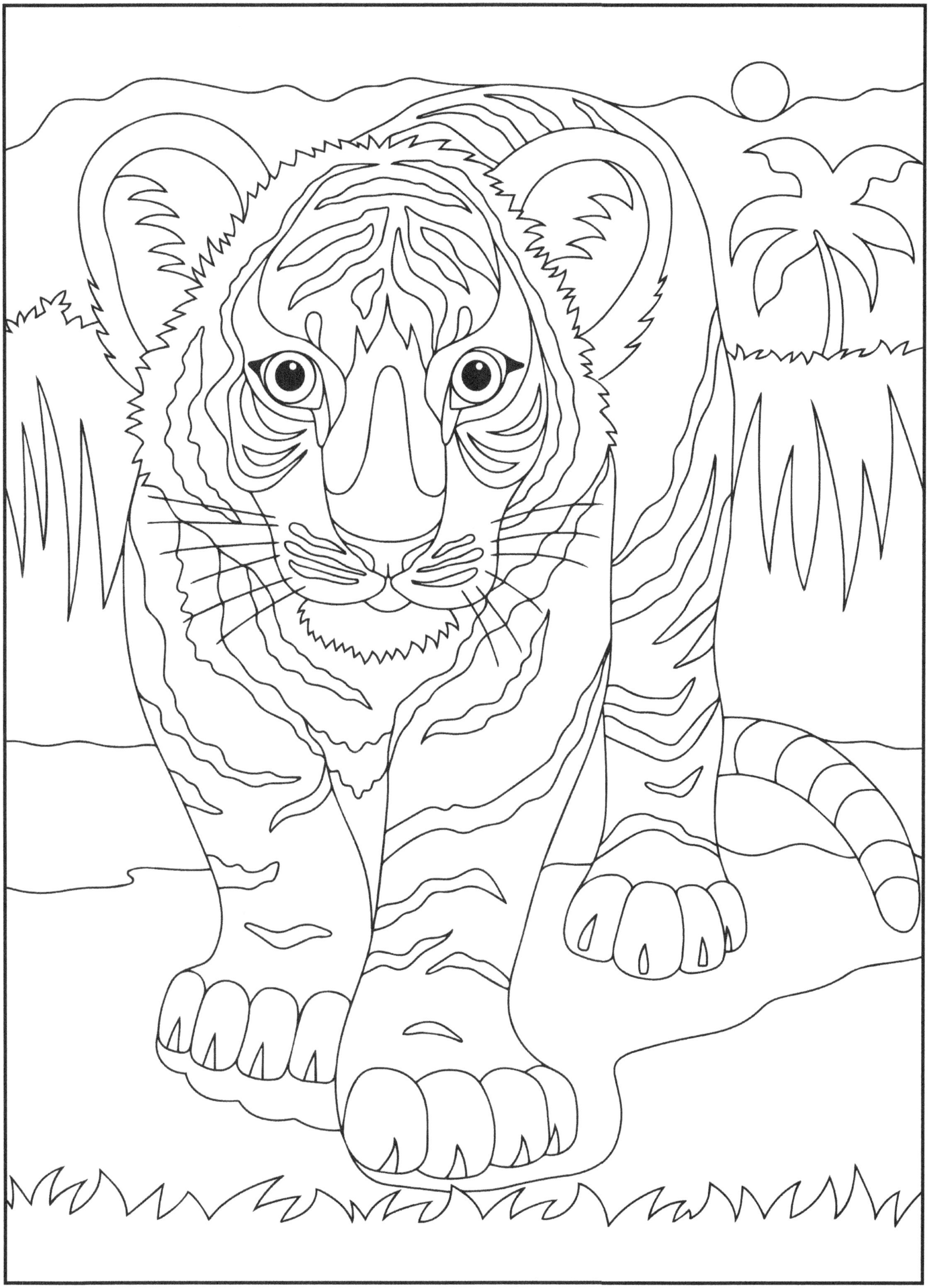

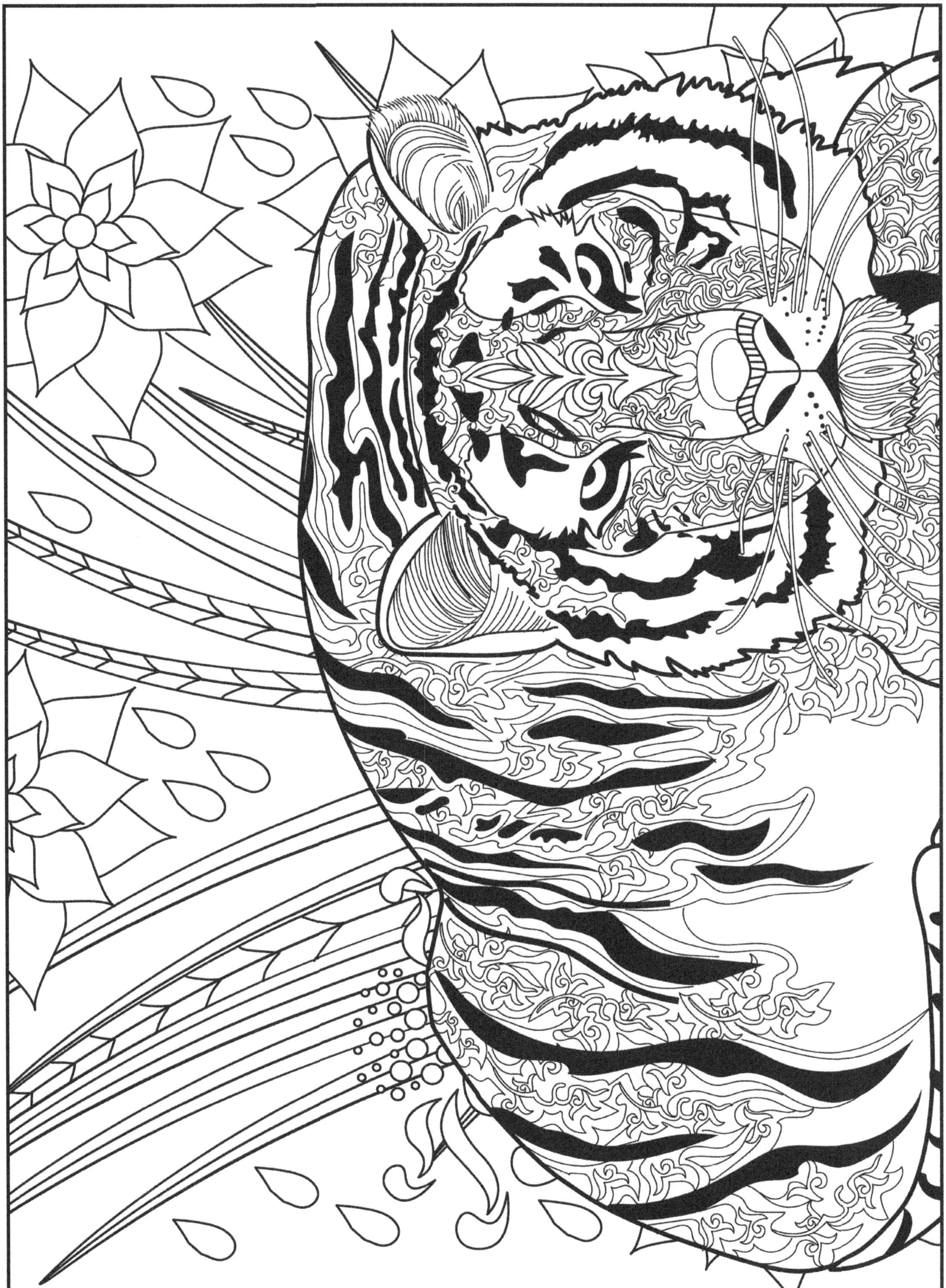

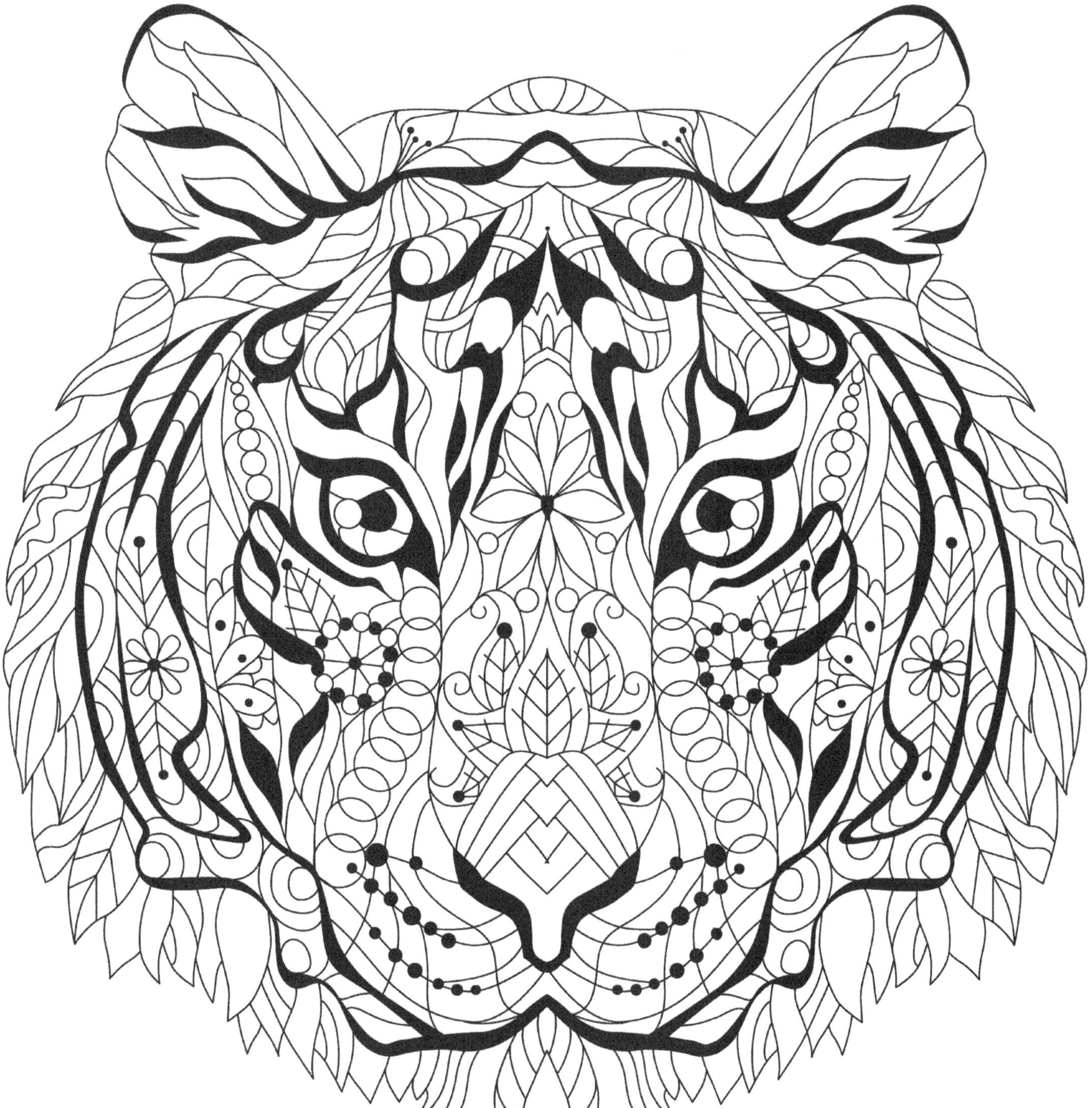

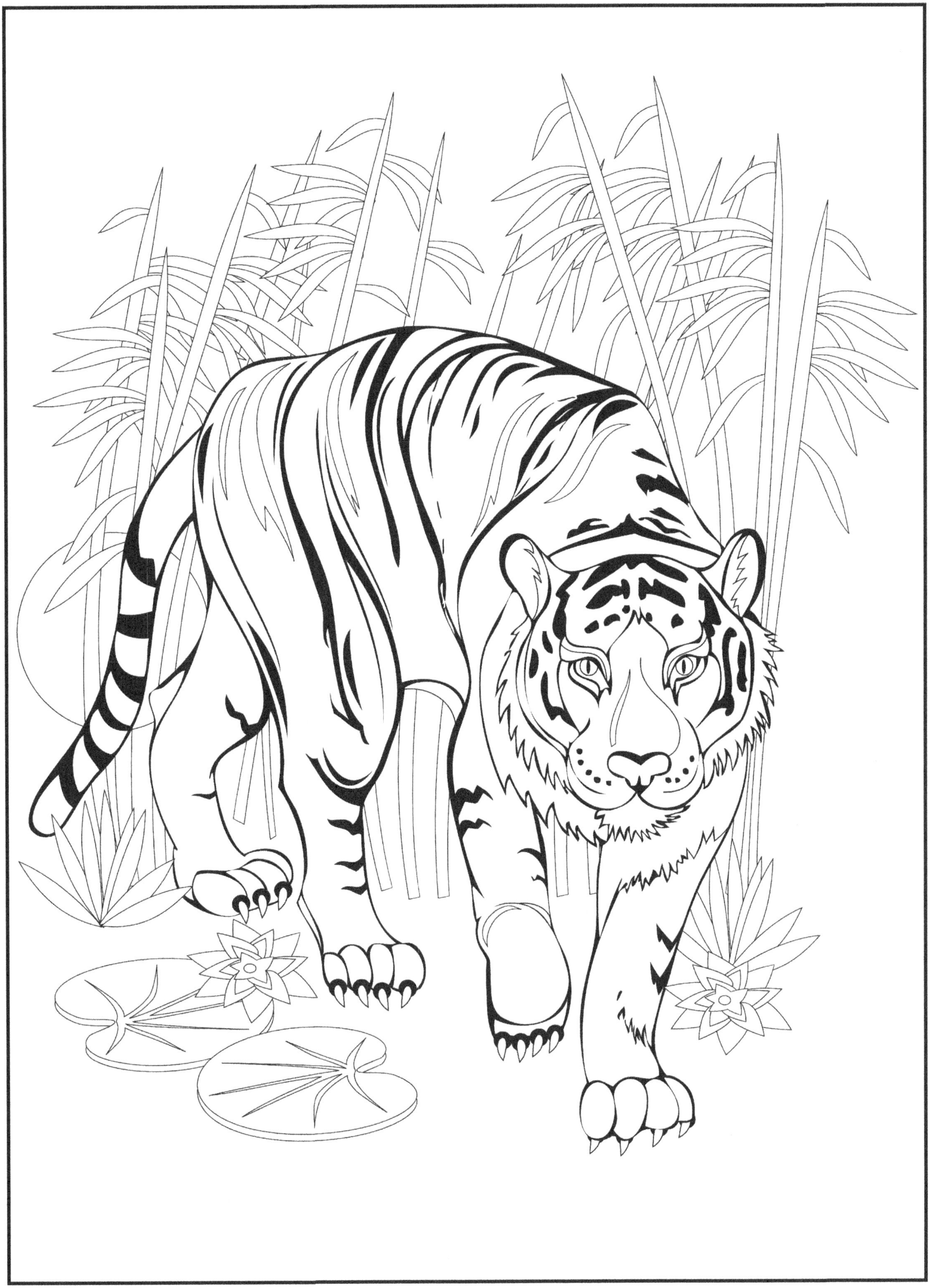

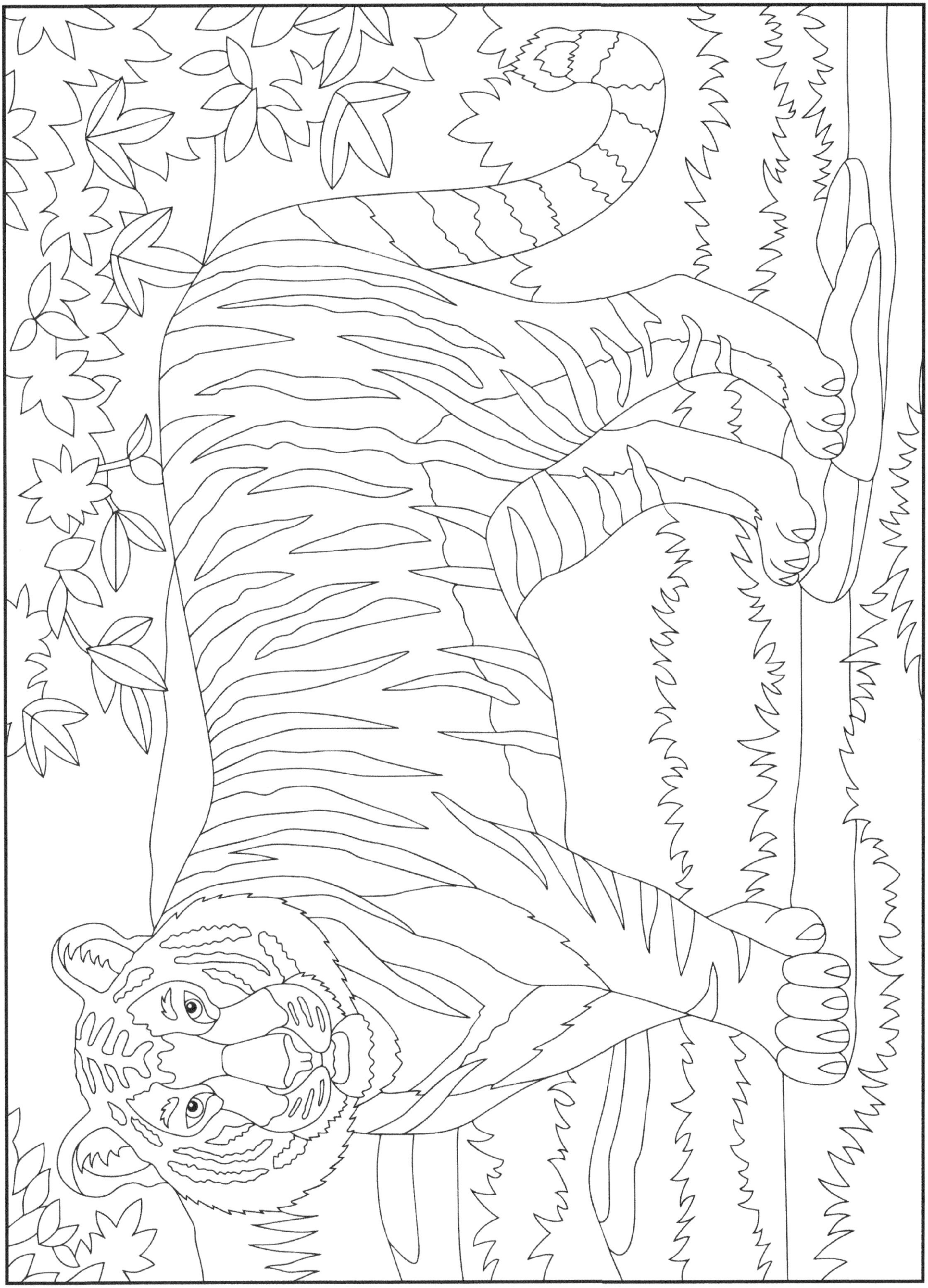

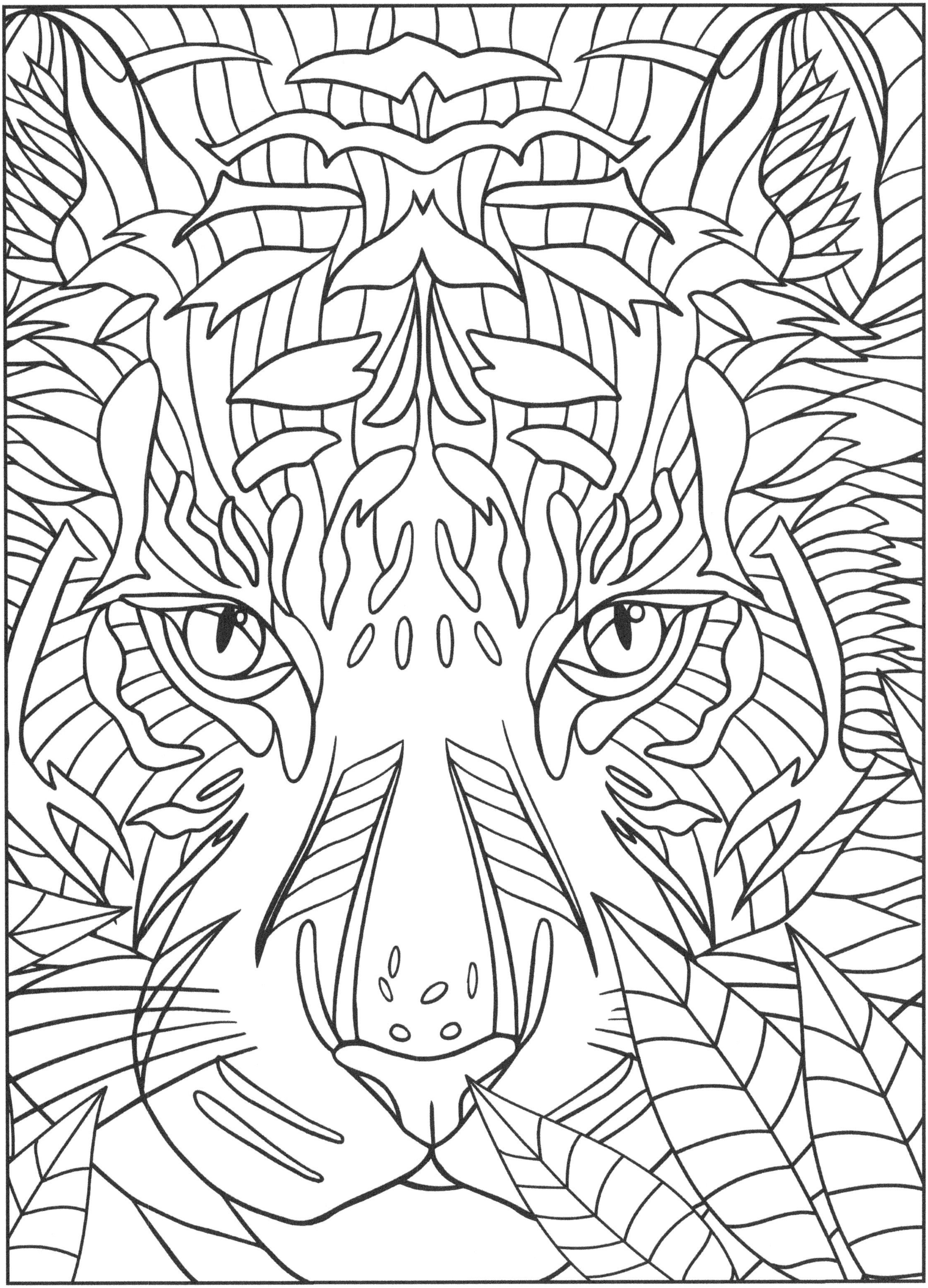

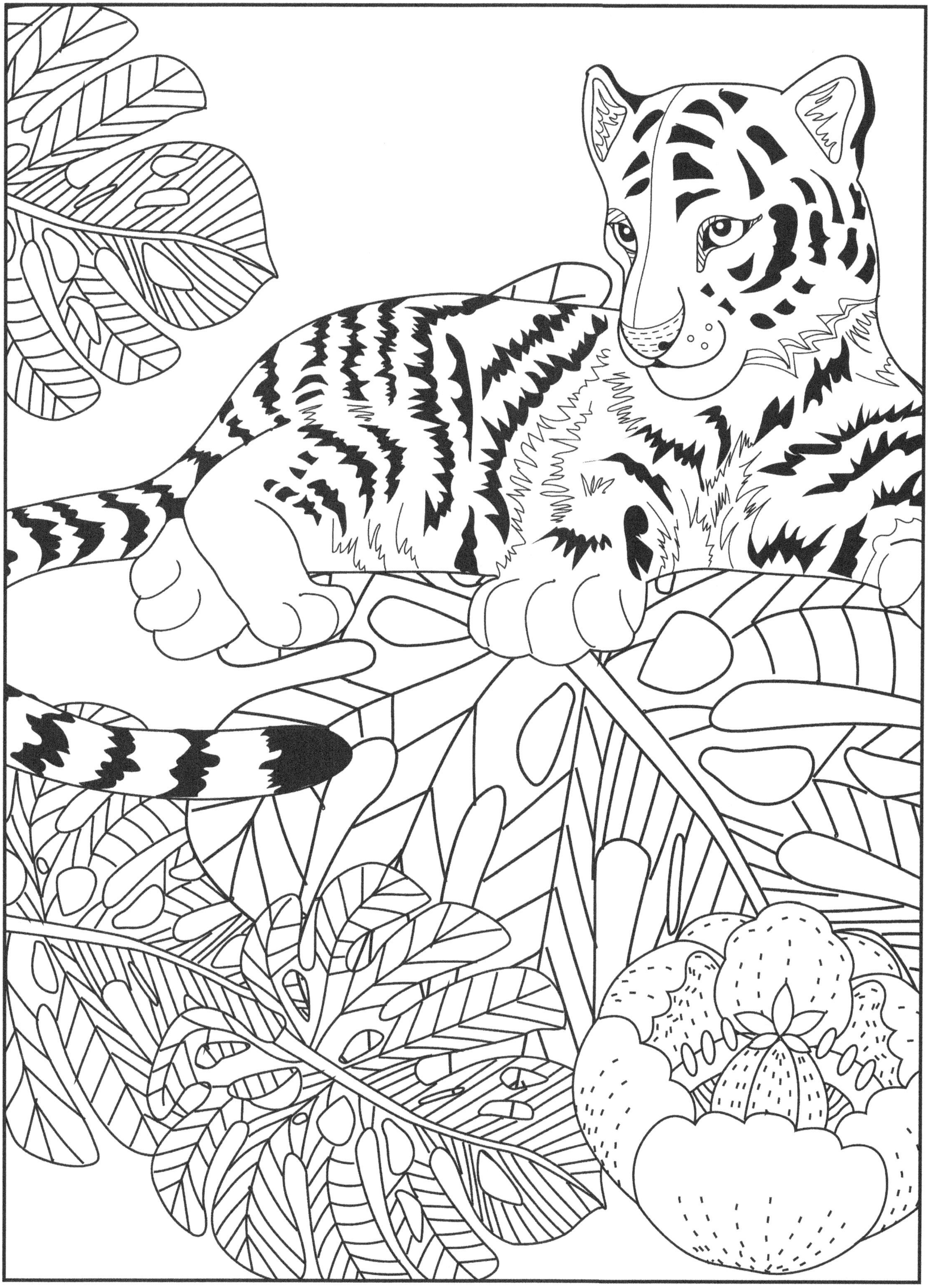

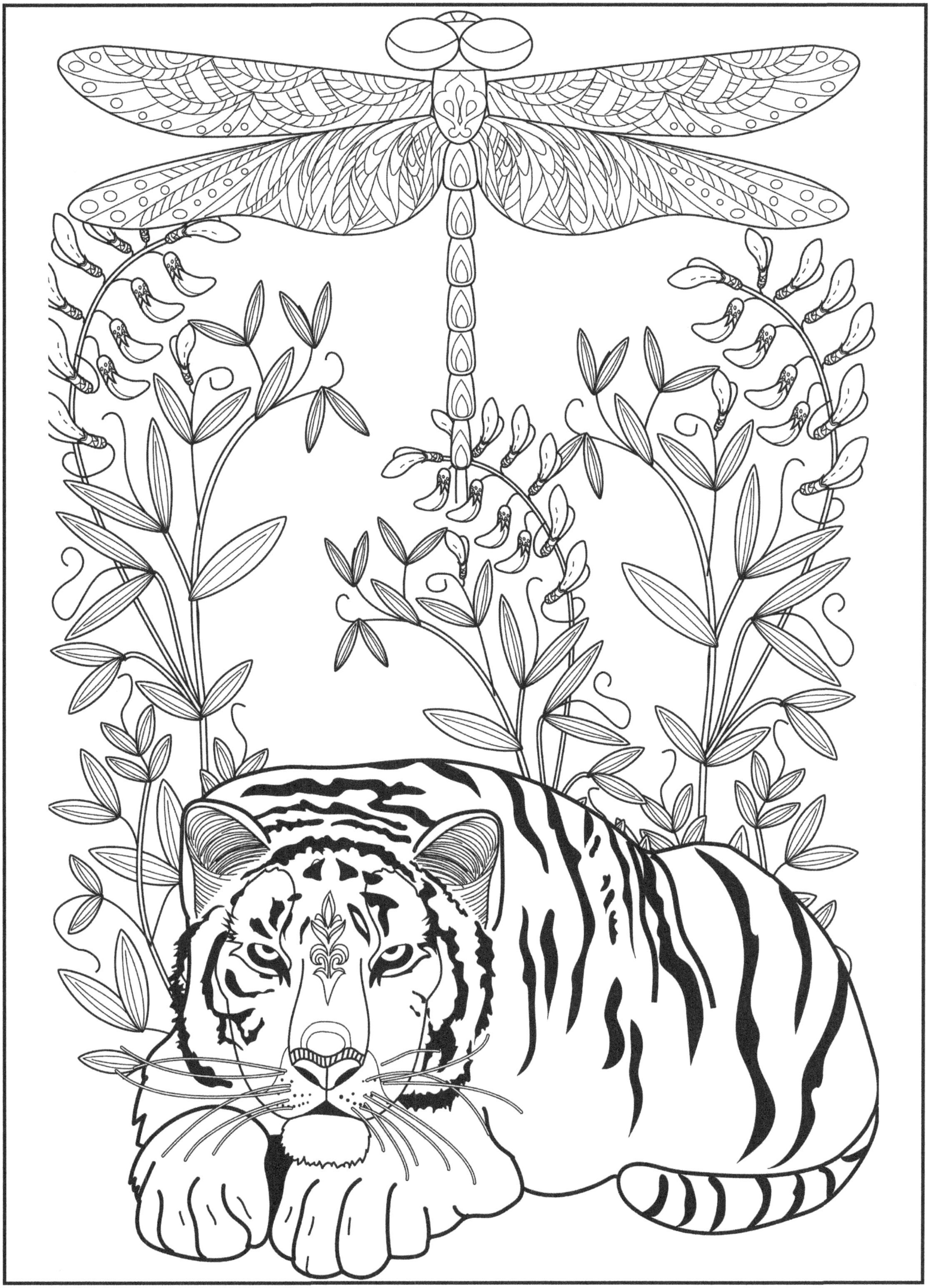

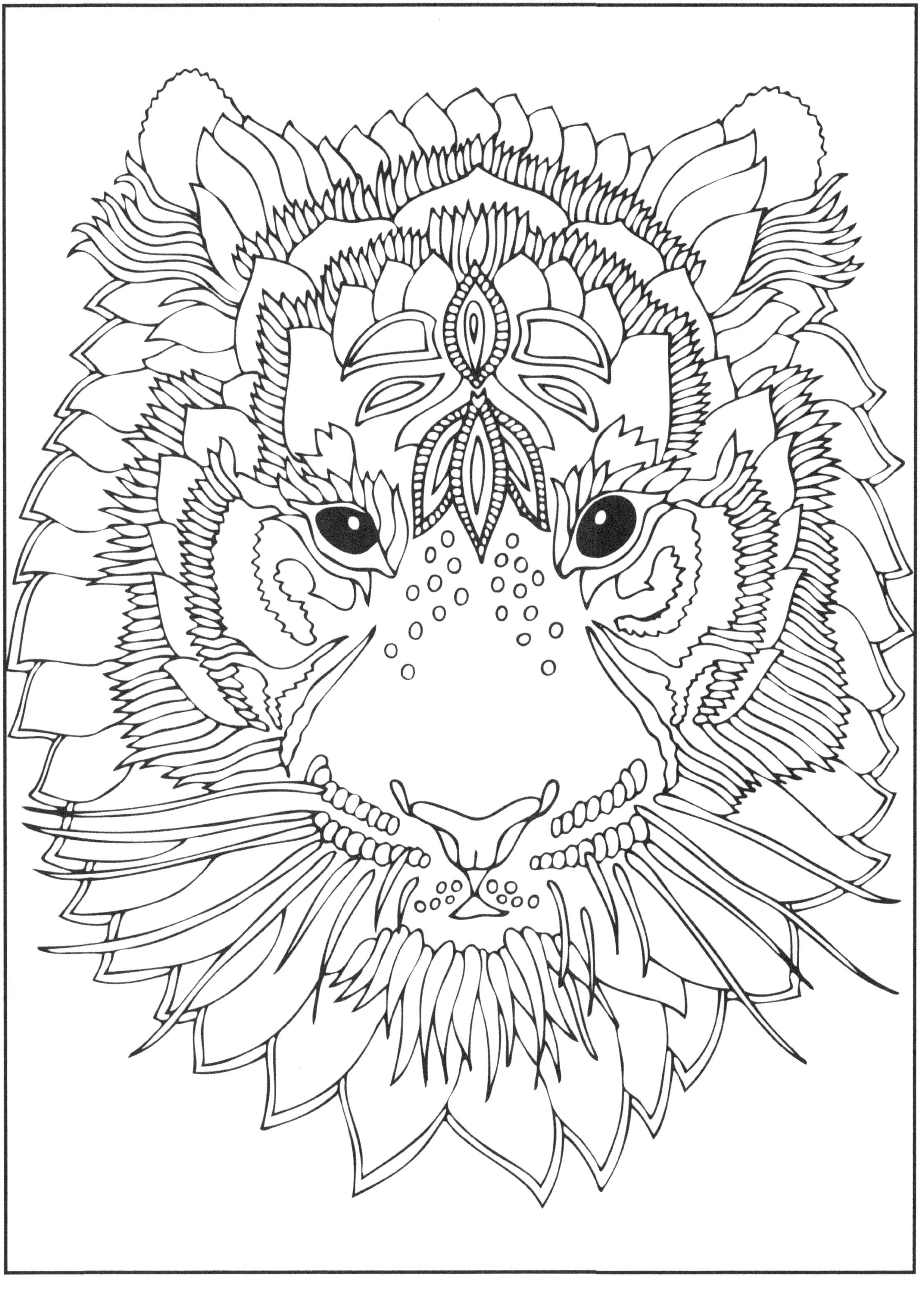

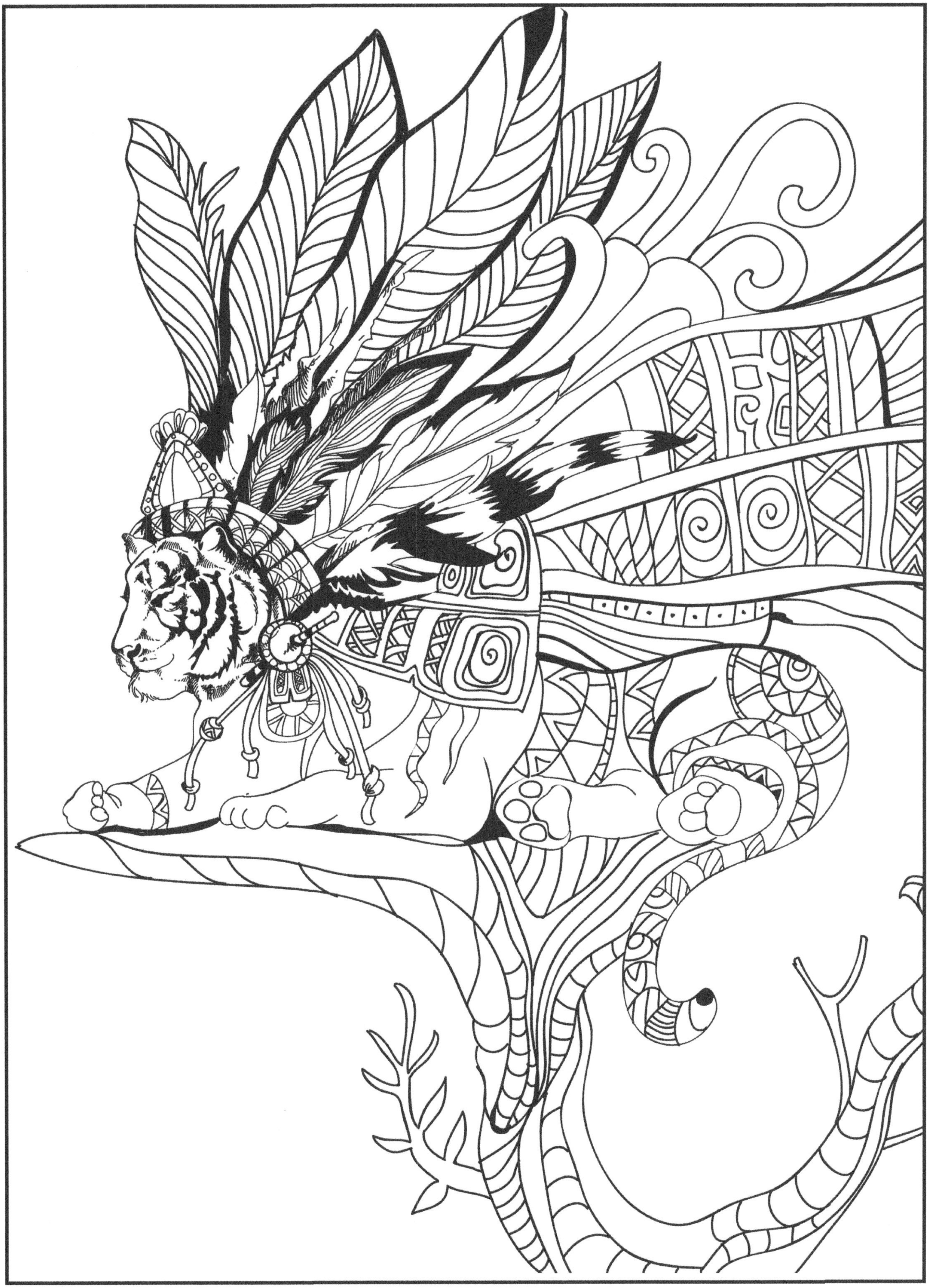

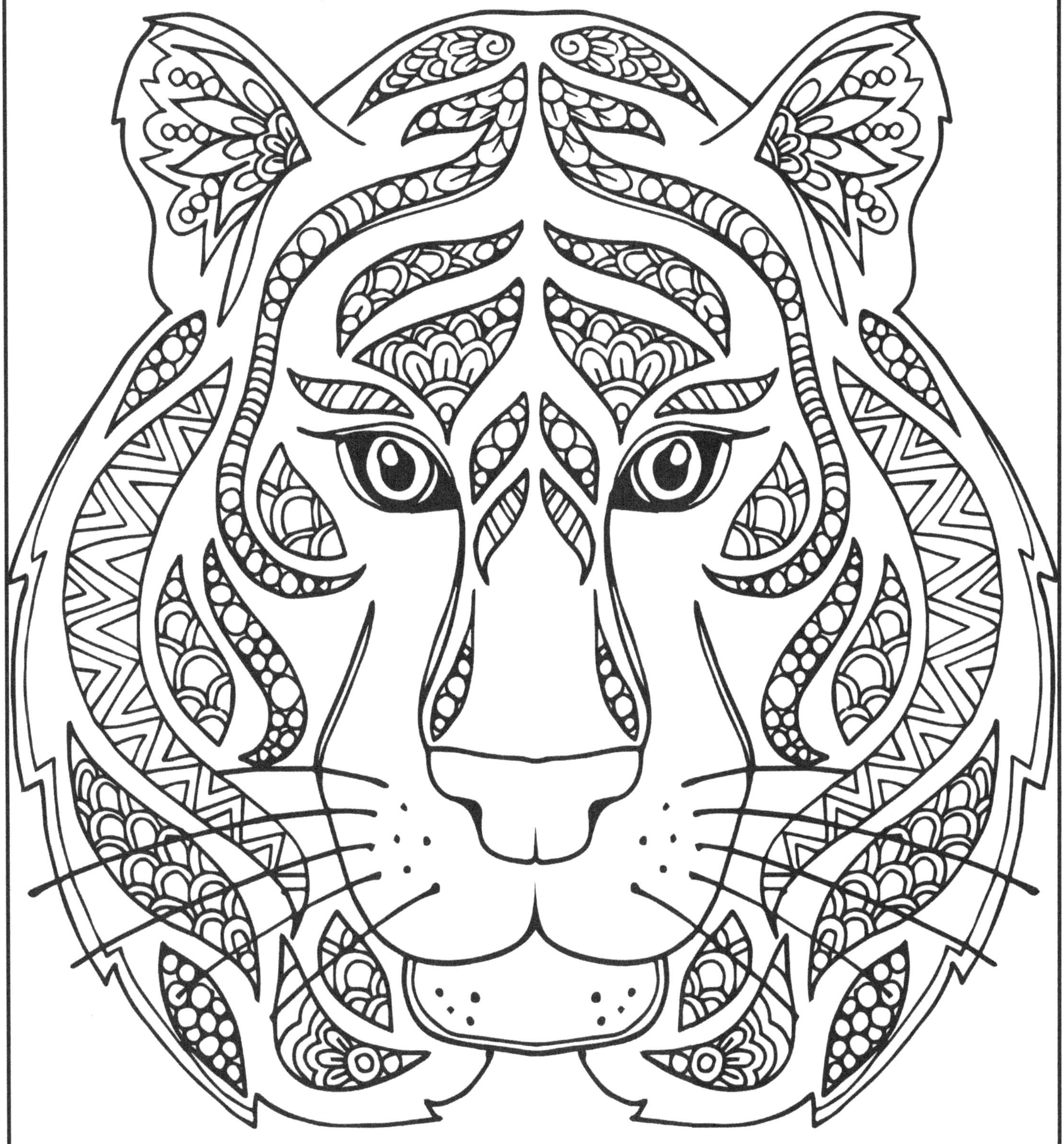

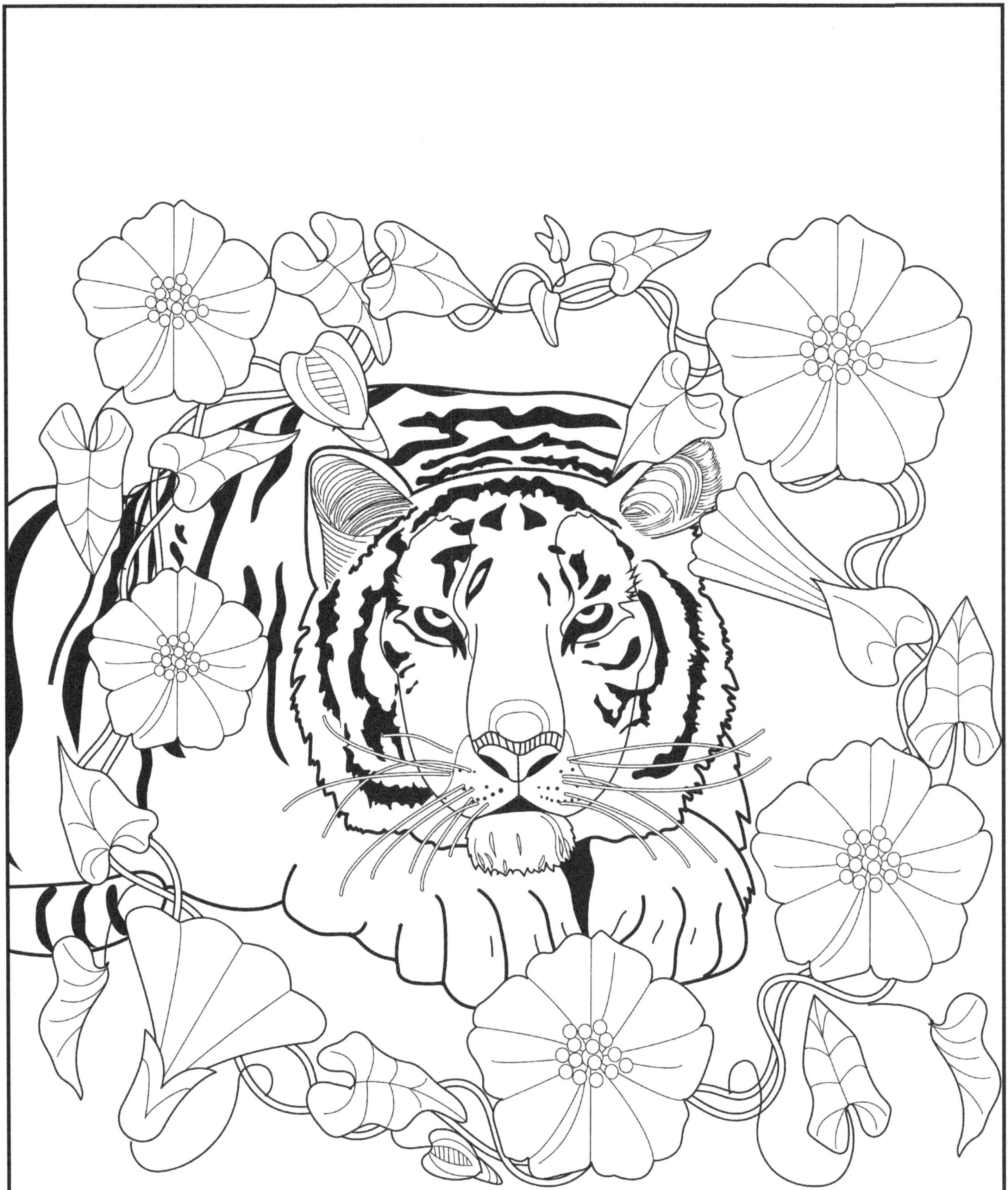

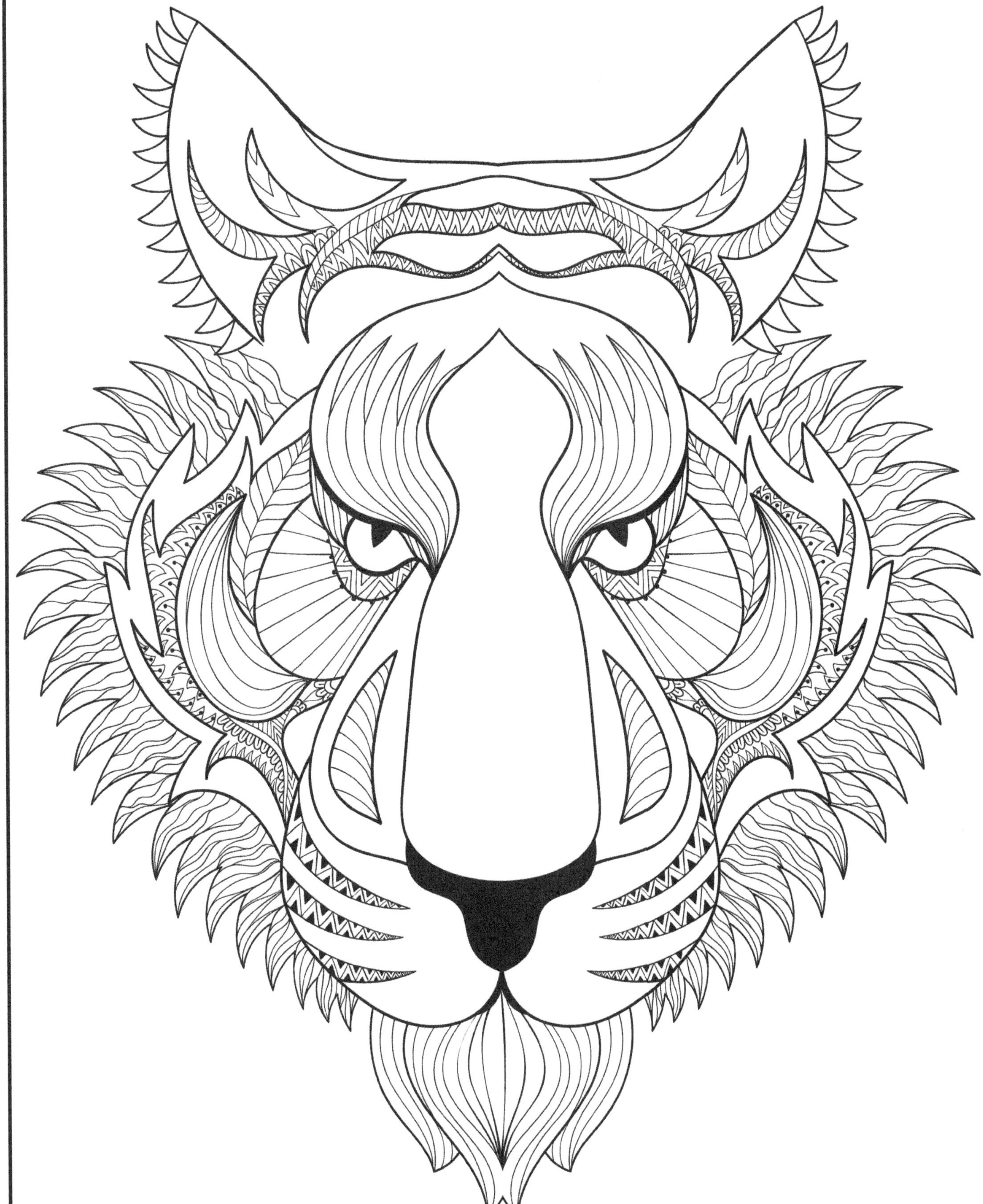

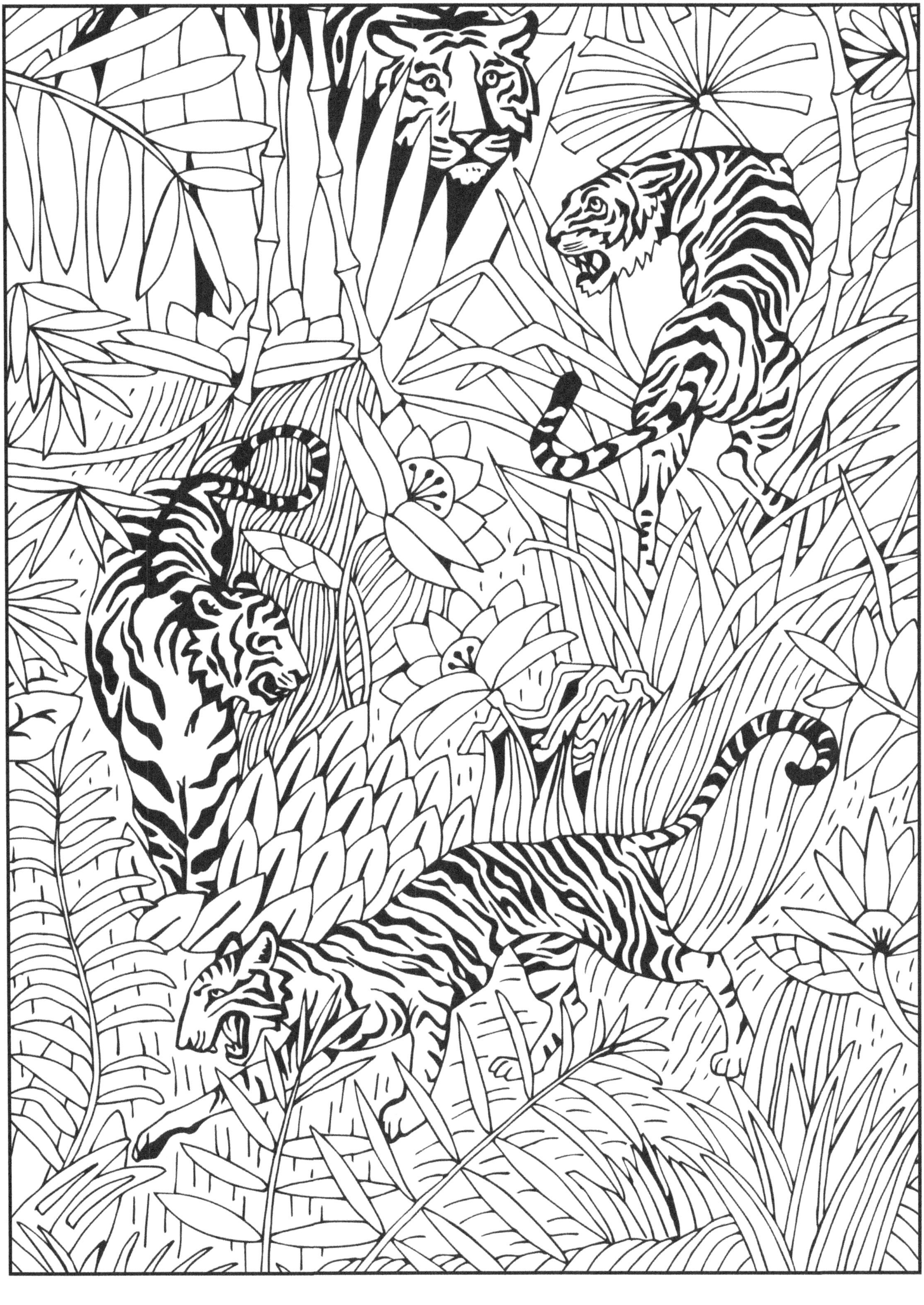

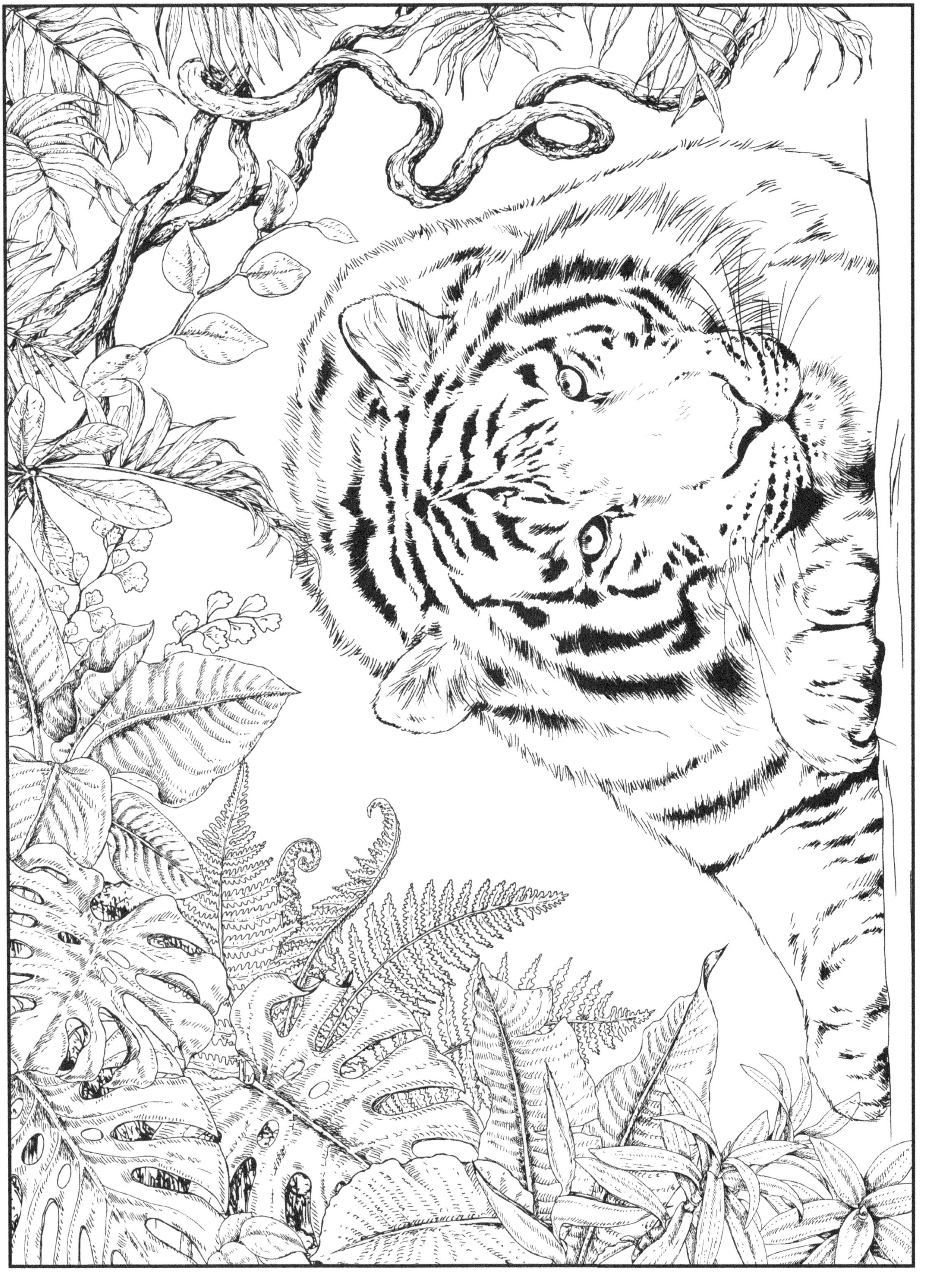

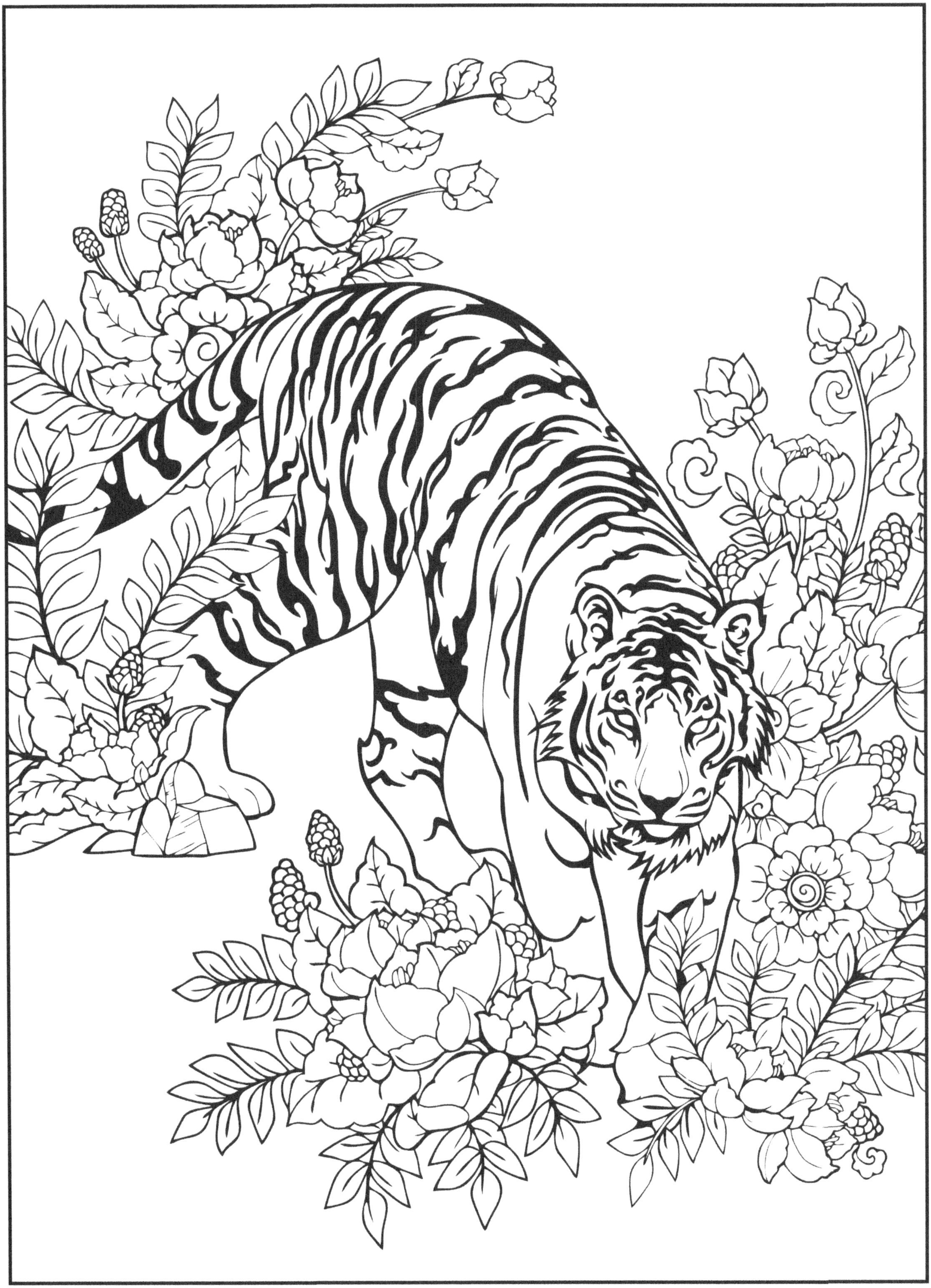

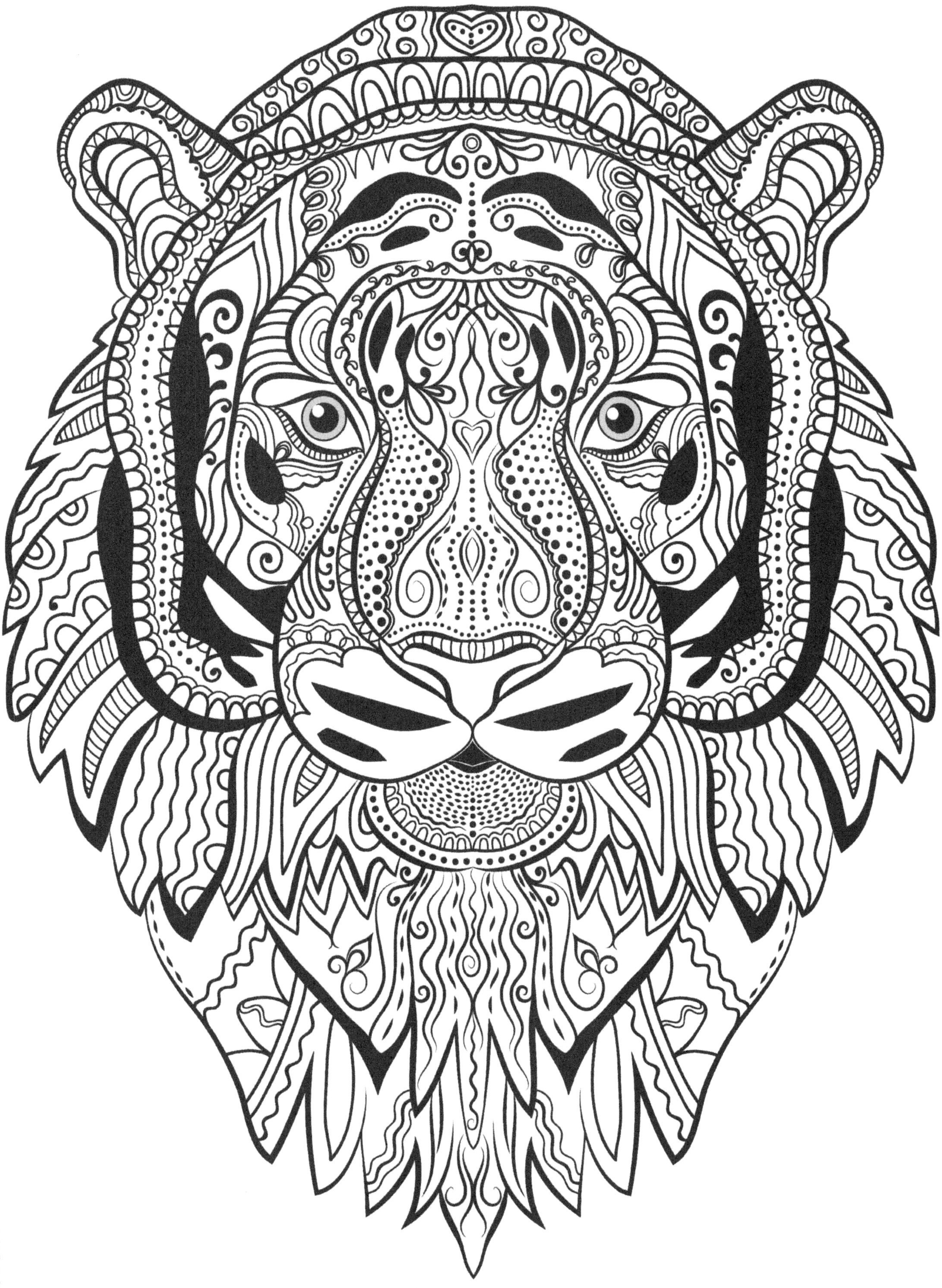

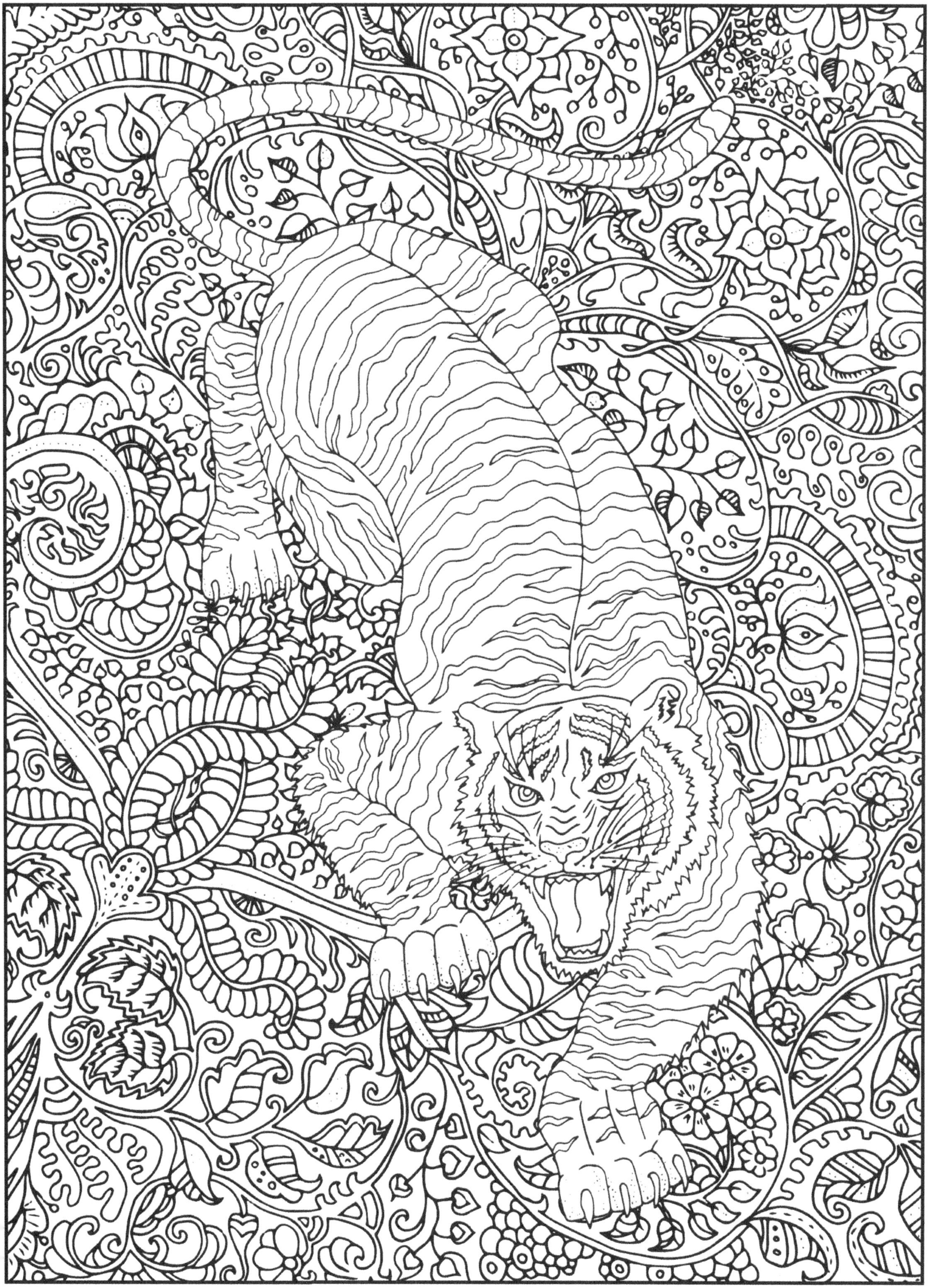

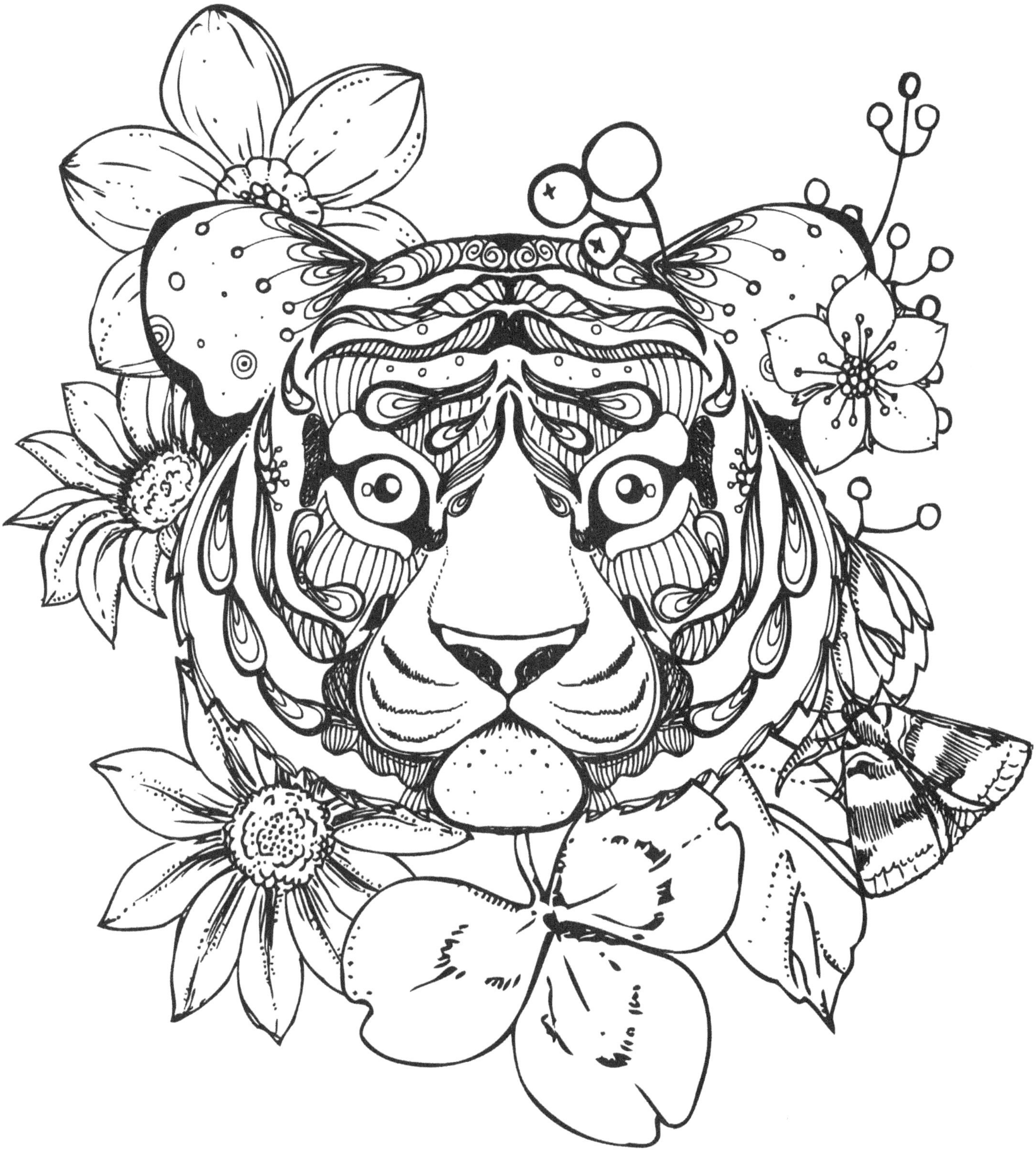

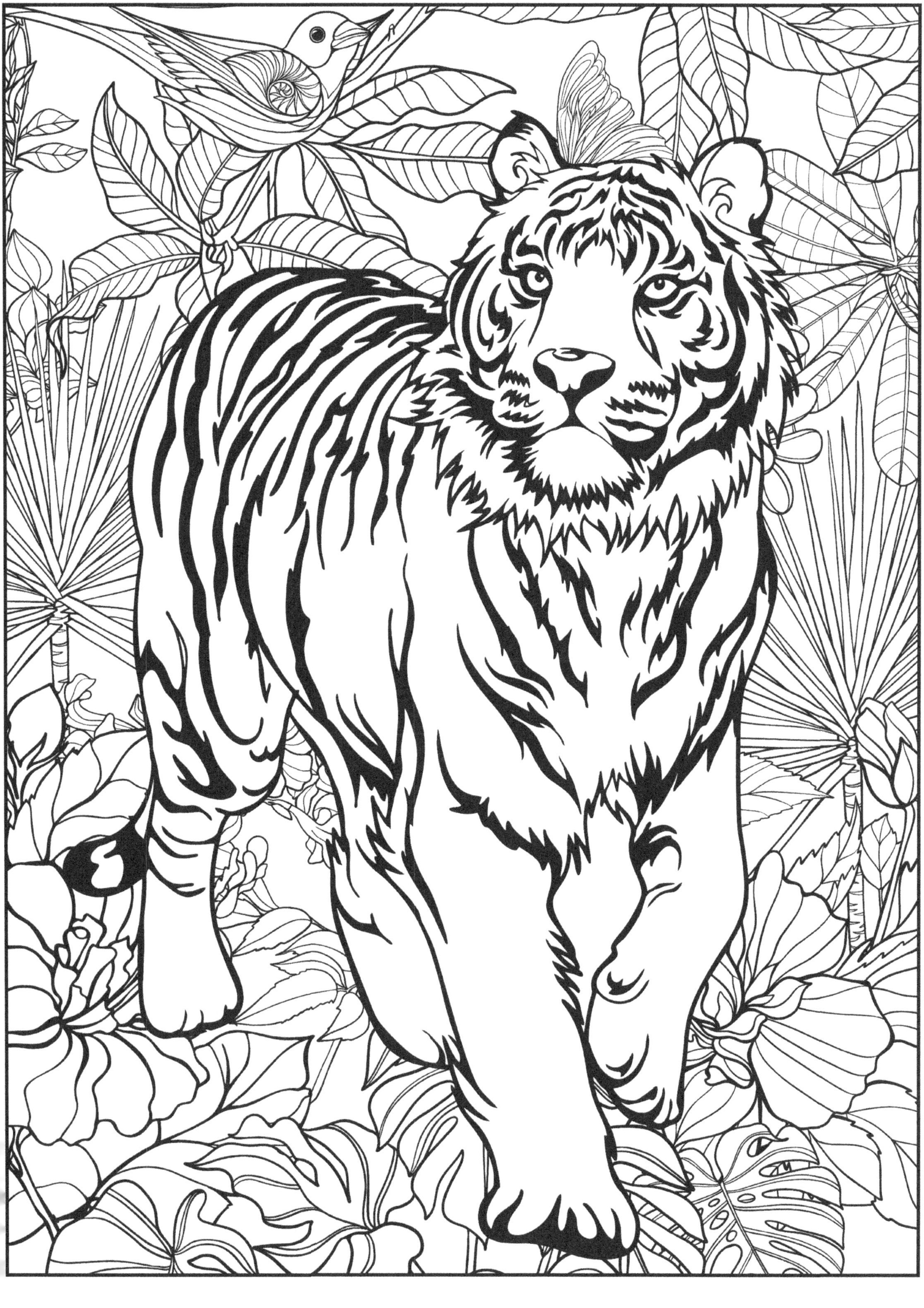

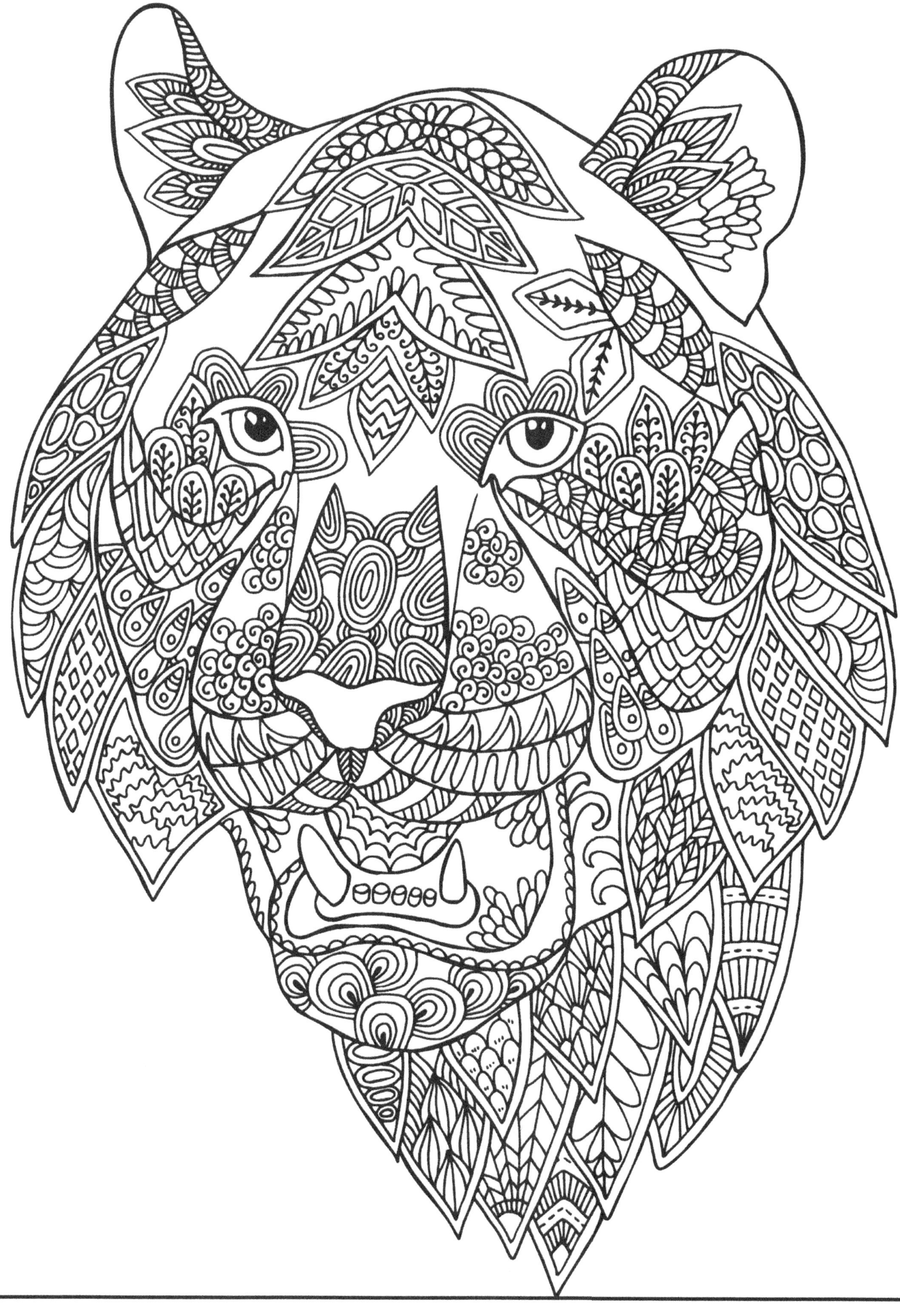

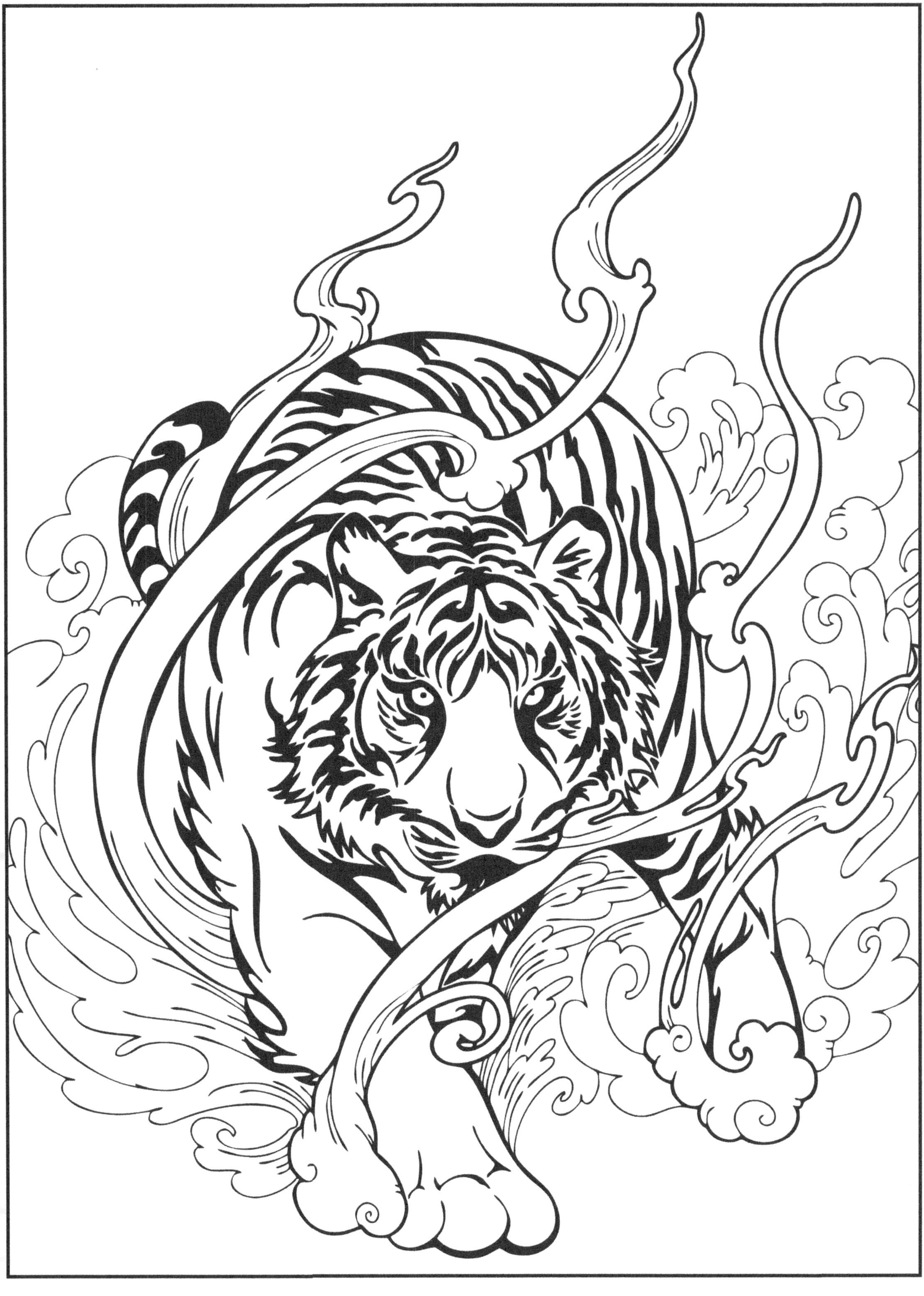

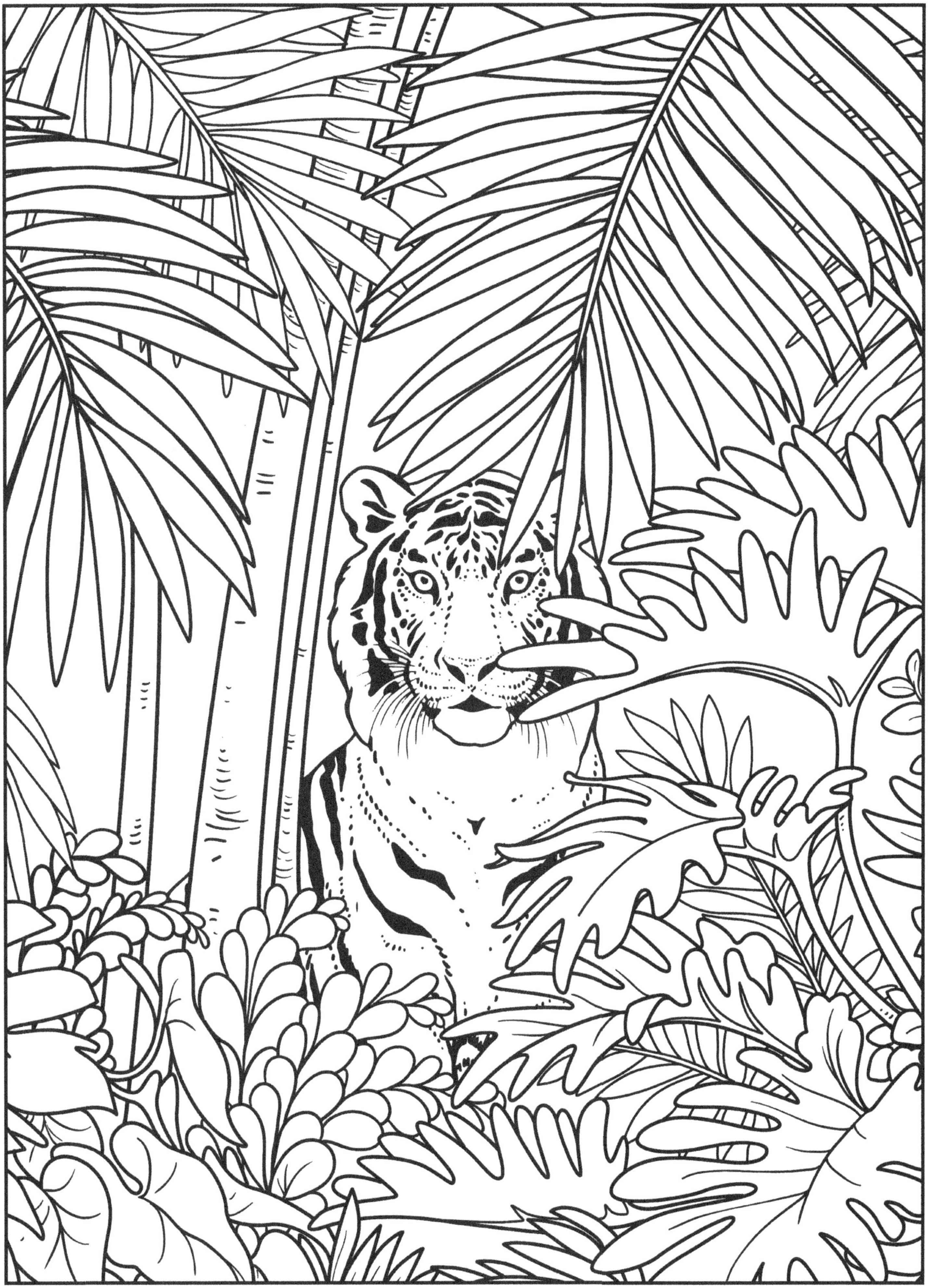

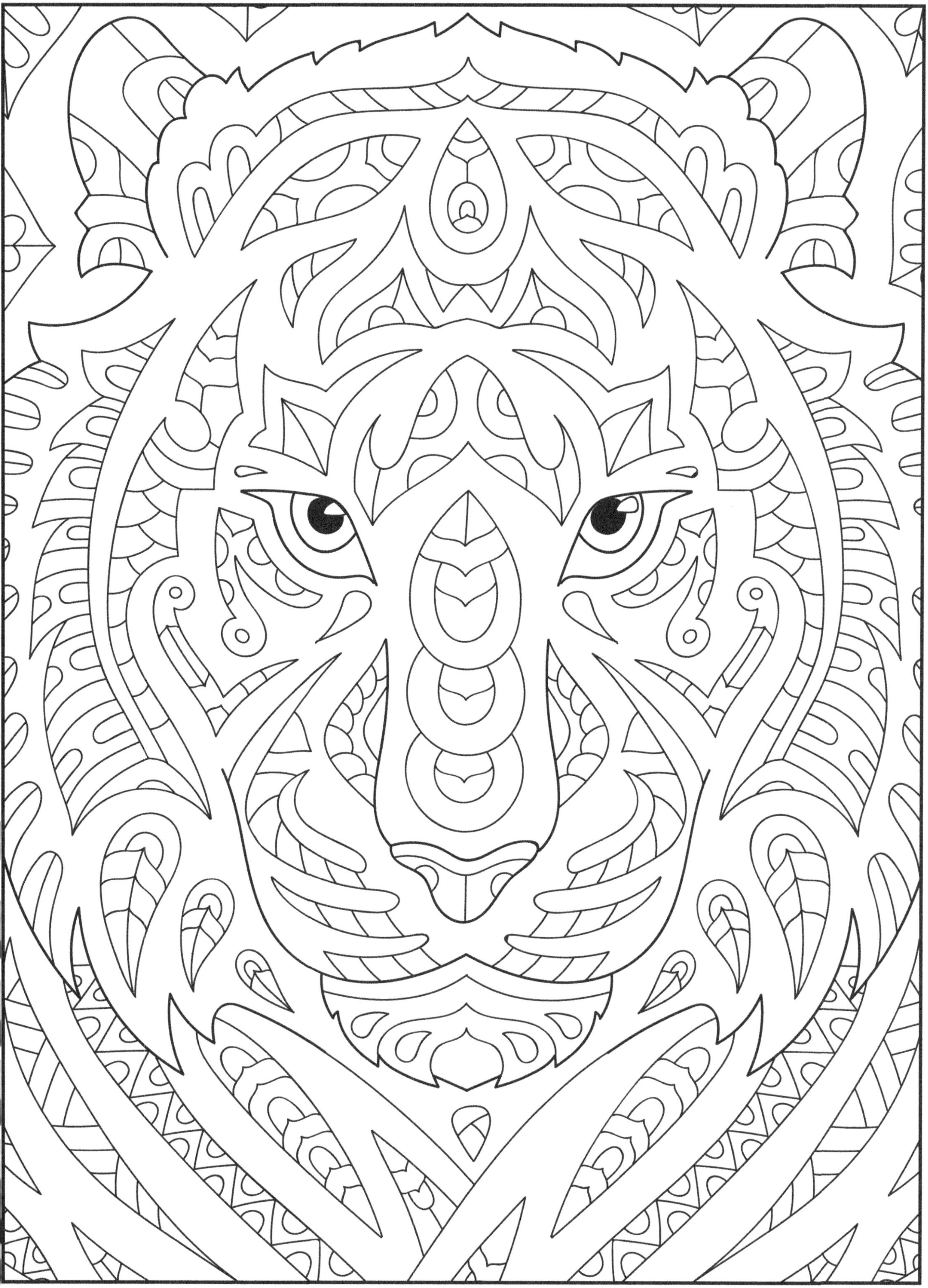

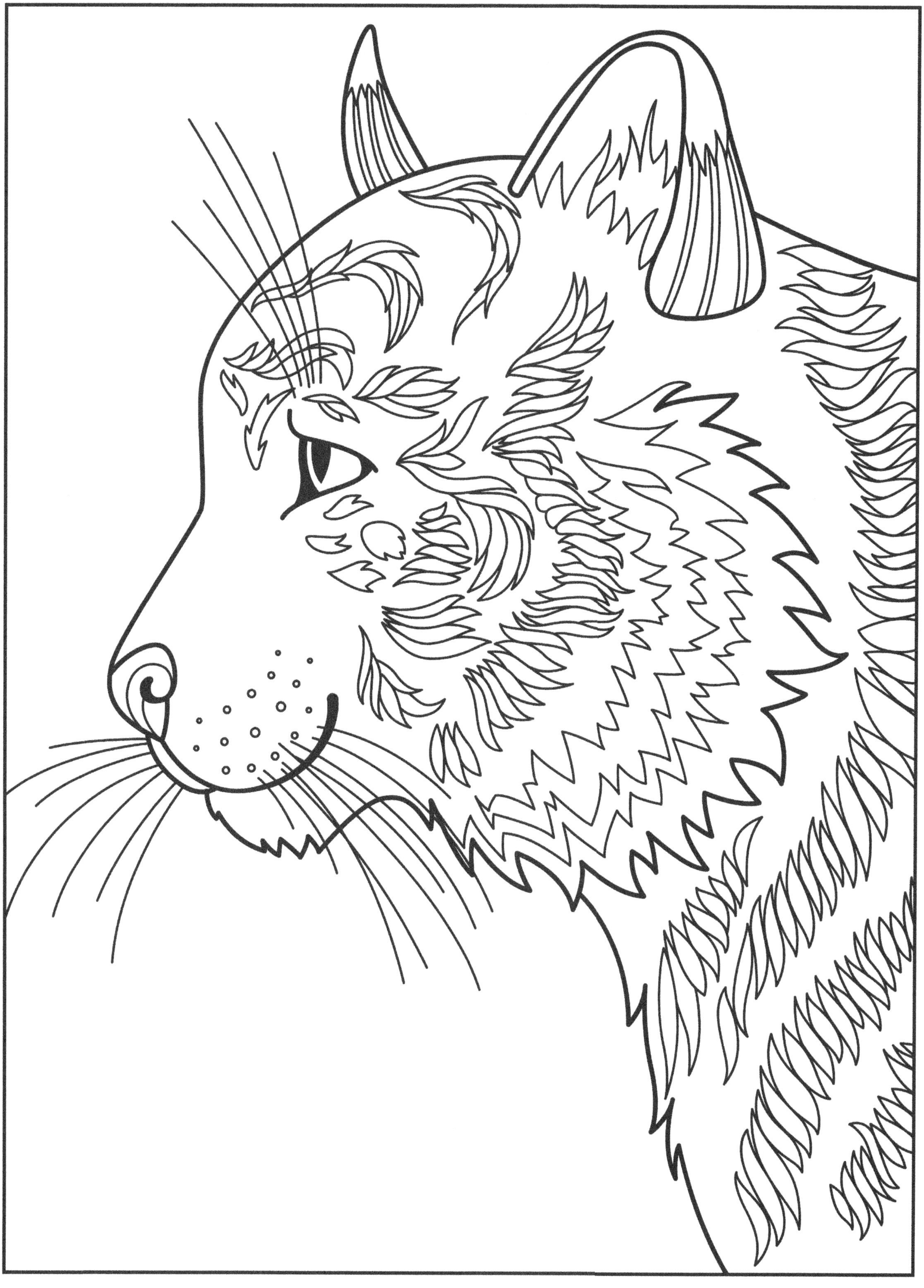

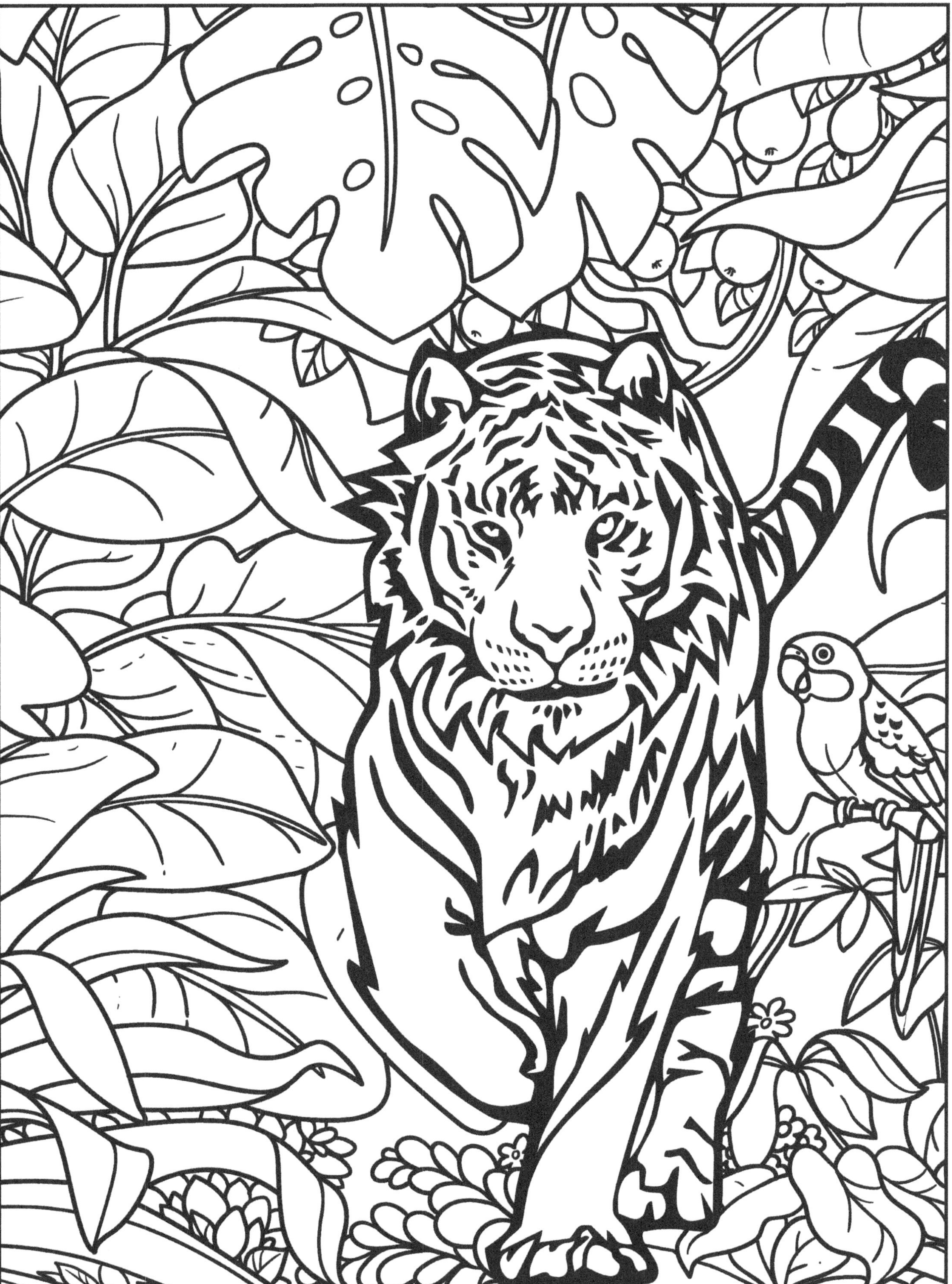

Made in United States
North Haven, CT
15 July 2024

54850699R00037